Reconstructing Sustainability Science

The growing urgency, complexity and 'wickedness' of sustainability problems – from climate change and biodiversity loss to ecosystem degradation and persistent poverty and inequality – present fundamental challenges to the production and use of scientific knowledge. While there is little doubt that science has a crucial role to play in our ability to pursue sustainability goals, critical questions remain as to how to organize research most effectively and connect it to actions that advance social and natural well-being.

Drawing on interviews with leading sustainability scientists, this book examines how researchers in the emerging, interdisciplinary field of sustainability science are attempting to define sustainability, establish research agendas and link the knowledge they produce to societal action. Pairing these insights with case studies of innovative sustainability research centres, the book reformulates the sustainability science research agenda and its relationship to decision-making and social action. It repositions the field as a 'science of design' that aims to enrich public reasoning and deliberation while also working to generate social and technological innovations for a more sustainable future.

This timely book gives students, researchers and practitioners a valuable and unique analysis of the emergence of sustainability science, and both the opportunities and barriers faced by scientific efforts to contribute to a more sustainable world.

Thaddeus R. Miller is Assistant Professor at the Nohad A. Toulan School of Urban Studies and Planning and a Faculty Fellow at the Institute for Sustainable Solutions at Portland State University, USA. He is also an affiliate of the Consortium for Science, Policy, and Outcomes at Arizona State University, USA. His research explores the social, ethical and political dimensions of science, technology and sustainability.

Science in Society Series

Series Editor: Steve Rayner
Institute for Science, Innovation and Society, University of Oxford
Editorial Board: Jason Blackstock, Bjorn Ola Linner, Susan Owens, Timothy O'Riordan, Arthur Peterson, Nick Pidgeon, Dan Sarewitz, Andy Sterling, Chris Tyler, Andrew Webster, Steve Yearley

The Earthscan Science in Society Series aims to publish new high-quality research, teaching, practical and policy- related books on topics that address the complex and vitally important interface between science and society.

Vaccine Anxieties:
Global science, child health and society
Melissa Leach and James Fairhead

Democratizing Technology
Risk, responsibility and the regulation of chemicals
Anne Chapman

Genomics and Society
Legal, ethical and social dimensions
Edited by George Gaskell and Martin W. Bauer

A Web of Prevention
Biological weapons, life sciences and the governance of research
Edited by Brian Rappert and Caitriona McLeish

Nanotechnology
Risk, ethics and law
Edited by Geoffrey Hunt and Michael Mehta

Unnatural Selection
The challenges of engineering tomorrow's people
Edited by Peter Healey and Steve Rayner

Debating Climate Change
Pathways through argument to agreement
Elizabeth L. Malone

Business Planning for Turbulent Times
New methods for applying scenarios
Edited by Rafael Ramírez, John W. Selsky and Kees van der Heijden

Influenza and Public Health
Learning from past pandemics
Tamara Giles-Vernick, Susan Craddock and Jennifer Gunn

Animals as Biotechnology
Ethics, sustainability and critical animal studies
Richard Twine

Uncertainty in Policy Making
Values and evidence in complex decisions
Michael Heazle

The Limits to Scarcity
Contesting the politics of allocation
Lyla Mehta

Rationality and Ritual
Participation and exclusion in nuclear decision making, 2nd edn
Brian Wynne

Integrating Science and Policy
Vulnerability and resilience in global environmental change
Edited by Roger E. Kasperson and Mimi Berberian

Dynamics of Disaster
Lessons on risk response and recovery
Rachel A. Dowty Beech and Barbara Allen

The Social Dynamics of Carbon Capture and Storage
Understanding CCS representations, governance and innovation
Edited by Nils Markusson, Simon Shackley and Benjamin Evar

Science and Public Reason
Sheila Jasanoff

Marginalized Reproduction
Ethnicity, infertility and reproductive technologies
Edited by Lorraine Culley, Nicky Hudson and Floor van Rooij

Resolving Messy Policy Problems
Handling conflict in environmental, transport, health and ageing policy
Steven Ney

The Hartwell Approach to Climate Policy
Edited by Steve Rayner and Mark Caine

Reconstructing Sustainability Science
Knowledge and action for a sustainable future
Thaddeus R. Miller

RECONSTRUCTING SUSTAINABILITY SCIENCE

Knowledge and action for a sustainable future

Thaddeus R. Miller

Routledge
Taylor & Francis Group

LONDON AND NEW YORK

earthscan
from Routledge

First published 2015
by Routledge
2 Park Square, Milton Park, Abingdon, Oxon OX14 4RN

and by Routledge
711 Third Avenue, New York, NY 10017

Routledge is an imprint of the Taylor & Francis Group, an informa business

British Library Cataloguing-in-Publication Data
A catalogue record for this book is available from the British Library.

Library of Congress Cataloging-in-Publication Data
A catalog record for this book has been requested.

ISBN: 978-0-415-63261-4 (hbk)
ISBN: 978-0-415-63262-1 (pbk)
ISBN: 978-0-203-38390-2 (ebk)

Typeset in Bembo
by Fish Books

To Britt and Zadie

'A new generation of students and scholars has embraced sustainability as a concept and is eager to explore more thoughtful, more integrative and better scientifically grounded ways to approach it. Thad Miller's new book is just what they are looking for.'

Paul B. Thompson, Michigan State University, USA

'Thad Miller's book presents a sophisticated, nuanced and insightful analysis of the emerging field of sustainability science. Particularly welcome is his analysis of the normative, ethical and epistemological underpinnings of different approaches to sustainability. His proposal for an explicitly normative solutions-oriented approach to sustainability is exactly right.'

John Robinson, University of British Columbia, Canada

'Thad Miller, in this new conceptualization of how to restructure for sustainability science, outlines the logic and mechanisms by which an action-oriented, outcome-driven science might emerge. His book serves as a guide for what all sophisticated future-oriented knowledge enterprises should have as a part of their teaching, learning and discovery agendas in order to pursue a more sustainable future.'

Michael M. Crow, Arizona State University, USA

CONTENTS

Preface   xiii

Acknowledgments   xvi

PART I
Constructing sustainability science   **1**

1   Planet under pressure   3

2   A science for sustainability   14

3   Constructing sustainability science   29

4   Tensions in sustainability science   46

PART II
Reconstructing sustainability science   **65**

5   Reclaiming sustainability: limits to knowledge   67

6   Sustainability as a science of design   79

7   Conclusion: sustainability and our socio-technical future   99

x Contents

Appendix A Interview subjects   104

Appendix B Interview protocol   107

Index   109

LIST OF FIGURES

2.1 Quadrant model of scientific research   17
2.2 The 'loading dock' or linear model of science and decision-making   19
3.1 Knowledge-first sustainability, socio-political and epistemic claims   38
3.2 Process-oriented sustainability science   40
6.1 Design imperatives   89

LIST OF TABLES

3.1 Boundary work and claims in sustainability science 41
6.1 Analytical focus, characteristics and objectives for potential
sustainability science pathways 93

PREFACE

In the spring of 2007, I was among a handful of graduate students to enroll in the inaugural class of the first School of Sustainability at Arizona State University. We had in common a deep concern for the state of our planet's ecology and its implications for human well-being, a desire to do something about this, and a collective excitement to be a part of a new program. Self-proclaimed guinea pigs, we eagerly signed up for this somewhat radical experiment in the reorganization of research and education to understand and address the complex problems of sustainability.

The School of Sustainability is on the bleeding edge of efforts to transform our research and education institutions to break down disciplinary divides and tackle real-world sustainability problems. From the University of Tokyo to Stellenbosch University in South Africa and, my current home, Portland State University, universities around the globe are shifting to reshape research and education in the face of rapid global environmental change. As they do so, they reveal the limitations of traditional disciplinary approaches and the barriers to transformative change in academia (Crow 2010; Miller et al. 2008).

In these changes and others, including the National Science Foundation's recent Science, Engineering and Education for Sustainability initiative and the International Council for Science (ICSU) Future Earth, there is a recognition that the ways in which we have come to organize research and education limit our ability both to understand and resolve sustainability problems. The challenges and roadblocks run from the seemingly mundane – such as how the distribution of student credit hours impedes interdisciplinary course offerings – to deep normative and epistemic divides between academic disciplines and assumptions about the relationship between scientific knowledge and social action.

Being a naïve yet willing participant in this upheaval as a doctoral student, I became interested in understanding how sustainability challenges were reshaping academic programs and emerging interdisciplinary fields. How are disciplines merging? How are the normative goals of sustainability incorporated into supposedly 'value-free' scientific research? How will the knowledge produced by sustainability research be utilized? How are sustainability problems framed? By whom? For my dissertation research, I took up these questions and others to examine the emergence of sustainability science – an interdisciplinary, problem-driven field at the forefront of efforts by the US National Academies of Science and the American Association for the Advancement of Science to address real-world sustainability problems. Sustainability and scientific efforts to contribute to it are rich territory for analyzing the complex interplay between science and society and how scientists are responding to twenty-first century sustainability challenges.

At the core of these and similar efforts is a critical question: How can science and technology most effectively inform and foster social action for sustainability? How is knowledge to be connected to actions and decision making that advance collective visions of natural and social well-being (Bocking 2004; Jasanoff 1997)? This book examines how sustainability science aims to contribute to social action for sustainability and the implications of emerging research agendas for societal discourse on sustainability. The results will help move sustainability science forward through a better understanding of how science might contribute to social outcomes more effectively. It will provide an opportunity to create more reflexive sustainability science research agendas and demonstrate the necessity of addressing the social, political and normative dimensions of sustainability in order to contribute to social action. I hope to lay the foundation for a sustainability science that is evaluated based on its ability to frame sustainability problems and solutions in ways that make them amenable to democratic and pragmatic social action.

This book has also been a deeply personal project. It began with reflections on what kind of student the School of Sustainability was trying to produce. How would we – those guinea pigs – be different? How can places like the School of Sustainability contribute to more sustainable communities? How will these experiments change the way we organize research and education institutions? These initial reflections transformed into my research agenda owing in large part to an incredibly fruitful and creative intellectual environment at Arizona State – particularly around the School of Sustainability, the NSF Integrative Graduate Education and Research Training (IGERT) program in Urban Ecology and the Consortium for Science, Policy, and Outcomes (CSPO).

After receiving my doctorate in Sustainability in Spring 2011, I accepted my current position as Assistant Professor in the Nohad A. Toulan School of Urban Studies and Planning at Portland State University. Portland State has made sustainability one of its campus-wide strategic initiatives. At Portland State, this effort is led by the Institute for Sustainable Solutions, where I am now a Faculty Fellow. Faculty, administration, staff and students at universities around the world are actively working to transform research and education to produce knowledge, technologies and people that will meet the challenges of sustainability. Arizona State, Portland State and other colleges and universities I've encountered in my research and through colleagues have met their fair share of barriers as well as successes. From this work and experience, it is clear that sustainability's 'wicked' problems (which I discuss in Chapter 1) present fundamental challenges to knowledge production and our ability to link research to beneficial outcomes.

This project is the result of empirical and theoretical research and deep personal and professional reflection on these challenges. It creates an opportunity for the emergence of a more reflexive sustainability science and demonstrates the necessity of addressing the social, political and normative dimensions of sustainability in order to contribute to social action. The ongoing transformations in research and education for sustainability throughout the world make this an especially exciting time to be involved in this work. However, the challenges are significant and carry risks for the students, faculty and administration involved. This book contributes to our understanding of the successes and limitations of such transformations and develops a pathway forward for a more radically interdisciplinary, solutions-oriented design science for sustainability.

References

Bocking, S. 2004. *Nature's experts: Science, politics, and the environment*. New Brunswick, NJ: Rutgers University Press.

Jasanoff, S. 1997. NGOs and the environment: From knowledge to action. *Third World Quarterly* 18(3): 579–94.

Miller, T.R., T.D. Baird, C.M. Littlefield, G. Kofinas, F.S. Chapin, III and C.L. Redman. 2008. Epistemological pluralism: Reorganizing interdisciplinary research. *Ecology and Society* 13(2): 46. Available at: www.ecologyandsociety.org/vol13/iss2/art46/. [Accessed 31 July 2014.]

ACKNOWLEDGMENTS

This project began as my dissertation project as a doctoral student at Arizona State University's School of Sustainability. If the dissertation process were not long and arduous enough, the long haul to this manuscript was that and more. Throughout this project, I have been incredibly lucky to have the support and cooperation of many colleagues, friends and family. Though long, it has been a socially and intellectually rewarding process.

First, I would like to thank all of those I interviewed throughout the course of my research for their responsiveness and for their generosity with their time. One of the highlights of my work has been the opportunity to meet such intelligent and dedicated individuals and discuss the core problems of sustainability.

This research would not have been possible without funding from the National Science Foundation Integrative Graduate Education and Research Training Program (IGERT), the Graduate Student Professional Association at Arizona State University and the Institute for Sustainable Solutions at Portland State University. This material is based upon work supported by the National Science Foundation under Grant No. 0504248, IGERT in Urban Ecology. Any opinions, findings and conclusions or recommendation expressed in this material are those of the author and do not necessarily reflect the views of the National Science Foundation.

The IGERT Program in particular and the opportunities it affords have been instrumental in my development as a scholar. I would like especially to thank the IGERT Principal Investigators, Stuart Fisher, Ann Kinzig, Margaret Nelson and Charles Redman, as well as the program administrator, Gail Ryser, for all of their help and support throughout my time as an IGERT Fellow.

As a graduate student at Arizona State University, I was fortunate to be surrounded by a group of intelligent, dynamic and committed students and faculty, particularly in the IGERT Program, the School of Sustainability and the Consortium for Science, Policy and Outcomes (CSPO). I would like to particularly thank the following colleagues for their input and support: Kate Darby, Ann Kinzig, Clark Miller, Tischa Muñoz-Erickson, Mark Neff and Zachary Pirtle.

I would like to thank my dissertation committee – Ben Minteer, Charles Redman, Daniel Sarewitz and Arnim Wiek. They have always been and continue to be available, responsive and supportive. Most importantly, I thoroughly enjoy working with each of them on this project and others, and hope to continue to find opportunities to do so in the years to come. Each of them set a high bar for scholarship, mentorship and friendship.

I would also like to thank the editorial team at Routledge. They have been incredibly supportive and enthusiastic about this work from the beginning. In particular, I would like to thank Khanam Virjee, Charlotte Russell and Bethany Wright. I am also grateful to Steve Rayner, editor of the Science in Society series. I am truly humbled to be a part of this series.

Last, but certainly not least, I would like to thank my family for their support and enthusiasm. To Mom, Dad and Cam for checking in with words of encouragement and, sometimes, incomprehension. Most especially, my wife, Britt Crow-Miller, has helped me through this in more ways than she knows. Not only is she a great editor but, more importantly, she is tolerant, loving, supportive – and a great travel companion on research trips. This process has been long enough to see us get married and welcome our daughter, Zadie Avalyn Miller, into the world. And to Zadie – thank you for showing me what matters in life.

As usual, all faults are my own, and everything worthwhile is in part a result of working with those mentioned above.

PART I

Constructing sustainability science

Constructing
sustainability science

1

PLANET UNDER PRESSURE

In the spring of 2012, during a run of unseasonably warm weather, 3,000 scientific experts and decision makers gathered in London at the 'Planet under Pressure: New Knowledge towards Solutions' conference. Convened by the Global Environmental Change Programmes and the International Council for Science, the goal of the conference was 'to assess the state of the planet and explore solutions to impending global crises' (Brito and Smith 2012: 1). 'Planet under Pressure' was timed to deliver a powerful message to the United Nations Conference on Sustainable Development, or Rio+20, to be held that summer. The 'State of the Planet Declaration', summarizing the key messages from the proceedings, was issued at the conference. The declaration provided a clear and urgent call to global action to meet the world's sustainability challenges. New scientific understandings of the Earth system, it declares, 'demand a new perception of responsibilities and accountabilities of nation states to support planetary stewardship' (ibid.: 2). Recent research and the large-scale action required by society, urge the authors of the declaration, require drastic changes in political and scientific organization:

> The scientific community must rapidly reorganize to focus on global sustainability solutions. We must develop a new strategy for creating and rapidly translating knowledge into action, which will form part of a new contract between science and society, with commitments from both sides
>
> *(ibid.: 4).*

I begin with this brief dispatch from London to illustrate the ways in which scientific discourse and knowledge claims, particularly around sustainability concerns, are intertwined with socio-political and normative claims and visions of social, political and ecological order. This gathering of scientific delegates sought to bring the power of scientific knowledge to bear on the social and political barriers to achieving sustainability. Insights provided by scientific knowledge, according to the Declaration, are a cause to reconsider our ethical and moral positions. In this case, a call for 'planetary stewardship' that requires radical changes to social and political organization to be put into practice. Both normative claims about what we *ought* to value and how, and visions of social and political order – 'interconnected problems require interconnected solutions' (ibid.: 2) – are positioned as stemming from insights gained through acquisition of scientific knowledge.

The Declaration contends that financial and political support for a reorganization of scientific research are necessary. Knowledge must be more rapidly generated and translated to social and political action. This requires a focus on solutions to global sustainability by scientists. They cite the International Council for Science *Future Earth* research initiative, which will 'develop the knowledge… for supporting transformation toward global sustainability' (Future Earth 2013), as the type of support and organization that is needed. Global sustainability challenges, then, should drive changes in research organization and priorities and to the more effective use of scientific knowledge.

Scientific discourse and knowledge making are inextricably linked to visions of social, political and ecological order (Jasanoff 2010; Latour 1988). The State of the Planet Declaration and the proceedings of the 'Planet under Pressure' conference demonstrate how knowledge claims about the sustainability of interconnected, socio-ecological systems are also claims to the proper social, political and scientific organization that is necessary to promote sustainability. These knowledge claims are also claims to norms and values that ought to be pursued and upheld. This relationship between science and society is not unique to the sustainability arena and has been explored extensively by science and technology studies (STS) scholars (e.g. Jasanoff 2005; Latour 2004; Shapin and Schaffer 1985). Science produces beliefs not only about how the world is, but also how it *ought* to be (Jasanoff 2004; Latour 1993). As scientists describe social or ecological dynamics, they influence beliefs about what dynamics are sustainable – what society *ought* to do in order to be sustainable. Scientists attempt to respond to social and environmental concerns by researching problems identified by society as important. How sustainability science influences the social, political and normative dimensions of sustainability may render the concept of sustainability and the problems it encapsulates more or less tractable in terms of social action.

Sustainability challenges are reshaping scientific research and education at multiple scales, yet global science and policy organizations and national and regional research and education institutions are ill-equipped to deal with integrative knowledge generation and the management of complex science – policy interfaces (Crow 2007; Reid *et al.* 2010; Miller *et al.* 2011). From well-established disciplines such as ecology and geography to emerging, interdisciplinary fields such as earth systems science and sustainability science, scientists are moving to find ways to contribute more directly to the resolution of society's most pressing problems (Lubchenco 1998; NRC 1999). Central to these efforts is the following question: How can science and technology inform and foster social action for sustainability?

Or, put slightly differently, how is scientific knowledge to be connected to actions and decision making that advance our visions of natural and social well-being?

This question has spawned a variety of efforts by members of the scientific community to contribute to the resolution of pressing social and environmental problems (Lubchenco 1998; NRC 1999; Palmer *et al.* 2005; Reid *et al.* 2010). Perhaps the most prominent and wide-ranging of these efforts, and the one that this book will focus on, has been sustainability science – an interdisciplinary, problem-driven field that addresses fundamental questions on human – environment interactions (Clark 2007; Clark and Dickson 2003; Kates *et al.* 2001; Levin and Clark 2010). Sustainability scientists aim to support sustainability transitions by linking scientific knowledge to societal action (Cash *et al.* 2003; Clark and Dickson 2003). The field is both problem-oriented and 'focus[ed]… on understanding the complex dynamics that arise from interactions between human and environmental systems' (Clark 2007: 1737). Carpenter *et al.* (2009: 1305) note that sustainability science 'is motivated by fundamental questions about interactions of nature and society as well as compelling and urgent social needs.' They define progress in sustainability science as those areas where 'scientific inquiry and practical application are comingled.' Carpenter *et al.* (2009) go on to stress 'the urgency and importance of an accelerated effort to understand the dynamics of coupled human – natural systems.' This argument is representative of a major theme in sustainability science: The fundamental understanding of the dynamics of human – environment interactions (e.g. Turner *et al.* 2003a,b).

Sustainability and scientific efforts to contribute to it are rich territory for analyzing the complex interplay between science and society and examining how scientists are responding to twenty-first century sustainability challenges. This analysis, then, will provide insight into how to develop a more effective role for science in pursuing sustainability goals. Utilizing theories and insights from STS, this book explores the construction of a new, and to some, radically inter-disciplinary, use-inspired field of scientific research – sustainability science. Sustainability science provides an important window through which to examine how scientific knowledge production – its organization and institutions – are being (re)shaped to respond to complex, urgent and value-laden problems related to sustainability. Through interviews and discourse analysis, I explore how sustainability scientists perform boundary work (Gieryn 1983), establishing credibility and epistemic claims and demarcating areas of normative and socio-political concern. This will contribute to STS analyses of the relationship between science and society as well as inform developments in sustainability science and allied fields. In so doing, the purpose is not to simply critique sustainability science, but to lay the foundation for a deeper dialogue amongst sustainability scientists, decision makers and other concerned stakeholders over the role of science in sustainability and future directions for the field.

This book will also explore the implications of transforming the contested and value-laden concept of sustainability into the subject of fundamental scientific analysis. Sustainability can act as a platform for communities to articulate visions of social and natural well-being, including responsibilities to nature and future generations (Norton 2005; Thompson 2010). In its broadest sense, one can view sustainability as an effort to formulate visions of the collective good. Science has, on one hand, brought many environmental problems to the world's attention, including ozone depletion, acid rain and climate change, which have in turn become the subject of normative and political concern. On the other hand, in offering objective and epistemically powerful explanations of natural phenomena, science can also constrain what is considered appropriate, legitimate or necessary discourse and debate. Exploring these issues, this work will contribute to our understanding of the complex relationship between science and the normative dimensions of sustainability and point to areas where dialogue may be 'opened up' to allow for discussion of alternative pathways to and meanings of sustainability (Stirling 2008).

Finally, I will explore the following question: How can science shift from identifying and describing problems in the biophysical realm to contributing to potential solutions in the social and political realm? It is this issue as well as the nature of sustainability problems as complex and contested that challenges the practice of sustainability science and its usefulness. In Part II, I develop a framework that pushes sustainability science toward focusing on the study and design of solutions, rather than the identification of problems. This is a new, explicitly normative vision of sustainability science that, I argue, will be more effective in advancing visions of natural and social well-being.

Before reviewing the structure of the book, I briefly discuss how the *wickedness* of sustainability problems presents specific challenges to the production and utilization of scientific knowledge, and how this analysis can provide an opportunity for sustainability science to address these challenges more effectively.

Wicked sustainability

Sustainability issues are often *wicked* – that is, they are problems the solutions to which are not obvious, wherein complexity is high, uncertainty is rampant, values are in dispute and trade-offs are the norm (Funtowicz and Ravetz 1993; Miller *et al.* 2011; Rittel and Webber 1973). Many of the problems that fall under the rubric of sustainability – ensuring adequate access to clean water supplies, developing alternative energy systems, evaluating intergenerational trade-offs in natural resource use, and advancing solutions to widespread poverty – not only are difficult to define but rarely yield to simple, one-time solutions. As the coiners of the term, Rittel and Webber (1973: 161) note: 'The formulation of a wicked problem *is* the problem! The process of formulating the problem and of conceiving a solution (or re-solution) are identical, since every specification of the problem is a specification of the direction in which a treatment is considered.'[1] Tame or benign problems, on the other hand, are those in which the goal is clear and it is easy to determine whether the problem has been solved (Norton 2005; Rittel and Webber 1973). Often, as we will see below, tame problems may be amenable to scientific or technological fixes.

Wicked problems are not just empirically challenging, they are linked to normative criteria (Fischer 2000; Hoppe and Peterse 1993). A central characteristic of such problems is that they are defined by value pluralism and that these values are highly contested. Consensus over problem definitions or the identification of solutions is very difficult. In the case of tame or benign problems, convergence on policy and technical solutions is possible in part because the proposed solutions can satisfy multiple value positions (at least for a time). In other words, wicked problems are just as political as they are scientific or technical. In order to understand such problems conceptually, we must consider how scientific or technical inputs allow for or impede the convergence of divergent and conflicting values on pathways that lead to resolution, even if it is momentary or unstable.

Richard Nelson's (1977) moon and the ghetto metaphor highlights why distinguishing between tame and wicked problems is critical. Though technologically complicated, landing on the moon is a relatively tame problem. The mission is straightforward and it is clear when the objective has been achieved. It is a matter of economic investment and technological capability. Success here is a testament to the capacities of science and technology to solve such problems. When there is broad agreement on the nature of the problem and what will comprise a satisfactory solution, science and technology can be powerful tools to inform our decisions and generate action (Allenby and Sarewitz 2011).

Nelson then asks, '[i]f we can land a man on the moon, why can't we solve the problems of the ghetto?' The problems of the ghetto are difficult to define and rarely give way to scientific or technological applications. How can we provide decent and affordable health care? How can high school graduation rates be improved? Addressing these issues is infinitely more complex. The solutions to such problems are often highly contextual and contingent on social, cultural, political and economic factors. In order to understand how science and technology might contribute to sustainability, scientists, engineers, practitioners and decision makers would do well to consider the degree to which a given problem is more like the moon or the ghetto – that is, is it amenable to a technological solution or does the problem lie in socio-political complexity? If the latter, are there elements of the issue that might be clarified with additional scientific knowledge?

This should not, however, be taken to mean that technological solutions are always overly simplistic or insufficient since they are perceived, particularly by the environmentalist community, as avoiding more meaningful value changes. In fact, as Sarewitz and Nelson (2008) illustrate, so-called technological fixes can be incredibly effective in enhancing human well-being and achieving specific and agreed goals. The challenge is not to avoid technological solutions in favor of genuine changes in values and worldviews; instead, it is to understand the problem context and what solution pathways – from technological fixes (which are rarely as simple as the critics would have one believe) to the long, but perhaps more meaningful, slog of social and political change – are most appropriate and effective in achieving desirable outcomes.

Many of the environmental problems that society has been successful in solving to some degree have been tame. Sewage treatment facilities and sanitation networks led to vast improvements in water quality and public health throughout western Europe and North America in the mid-nineteenth century (Melosi 2008). Likewise, the invention and eventual widespread use of the catalytic converter in the 1950s and 1960s substantially reduced the toxicity of automobile emissions, contributing to improve air quality in heavily congested cities. A key point is that these tame problems are amenable to technical applications that are relatively uncontroversial and help to settle potential value debates. This is possible because the goal is clear and does not involve significant trade-off between various interests (Lindblom 1959). For wicked problems, this process is not possible. Potential technological or policy solutions to wicked problems such as climate change often divide as many interests as they bring together. Furthermore, owing to normative and empirical complexity, solutions to wicked problems often end up leading to the proliferation of additional, unforeseen problems (Latour 1993; Scott 1998).

Yet it is also the case that, before modern sewage and sanitation systems, the problems of water-borne disease, water quality and public health were wicked.[2] This is an example in which a wicked problem was tamed by technological developments, political will and institutional change. Such developments can occur in the absence of necessary scientific understanding or even despite incorrect scientific understandings. For example, in the case of sanitation the miasmatic theory, which associated disease with bad smells, dominated contemporary thinking as new methods for sanitation and disease prevention were first implemented.

Additional scientific knowledge may not necessarily be the tool to help solve or settle a wicked problem. Calls for mode-2 knowledge production (Nowotny *et al.* 2001) and post-normal science (Funtowicz and Ravetz 1993) have recognized and thoughtfully explored this dynamic. In fact, additional knowledge will likely be contested by conflicting scientific findings or political positions and reveal additional uncertainties, rather than eliminating them (Sarewitz 2004). To what degree does sustainability science grapple with these issues? How do sustainability scientists navigate normative and epistemic issues at the science – policy interface and then address the social, political and ethical challenges posed by sustainability problems? Sustainability science serves as an example to explore how far sustainability concerns are reshaping scientific research agendas, if at all. If sustainability scientists are to facilitate social learning and link knowledge to action, they must be able to differentiate between these various types of problems and provide the knowledge or tools appropriate for a given context. This book analyzes how sustainability scientists currently approach these dynamics and develops a framework for the field that incorporates these insights.

Book structure

The point of departure for this analysis is itself an openly normative one – sustainability is a valuable and value-laden concept that may allow communities and society writ large to articulate and represent visions of human and natural well-being. In a search for a new path for progress, sustainability links concerns for the value(s) of nature, social justice and poverty with responsibilities to future generations. It attempts to demarcate a desirable space in which humans would like to exist; a path in which society should develop in a way that limits the negative human impacts (or even seeks to produce positive impacts) on ecological support systems, reduces social injustices such as hunger and poverty, and takes a long-term, multigenerational perspective. Sustainability is a normative claim about how the world is (i.e. unsustainable) and how it *ought* to be. Sustainability offers the potential for constructing a new and improved discourse for discussion of environmental problems because it is both descriptive and evaluative (Norton 2005). As Norton (2005) argues, it is a 'thick' concept that can encapsulate a great deal of information about how humans interact with the environment and present that information in a way that is transparent, important to widely held social values and helps move communities toward adopting more sustainable practices.

The book is organized in two parts. The first – Chapters 2, 3 and 4 – is an empirical and theoretical analysis of the emergence of sustainability science. Chapter 2 provides a detailed discussion of the theoretical and methodological approach taken in the book, drawing mostly from STS. It also provides a brief overview of the emergence of sustainability science. Chapter 3 discusses the results of 28 in-depth interviews conducted with leading sustainability scientists. This chapter draws from a content analysis of the relevant literature in sustainability science, examining how scientists are constructing research agendas for sustainability. More specifically, it addresses three core questions: (1) How do sustainability scientists define and bound sustainability? (2) How and why are various research agendas being constructed to address these notions of sustainability? (3) How do scientists see their research contributing to societal efforts to move toward sustainability? Following Thomas Gieryn's (1983, 1995) concept of boundary work, this chapter analyzes how sustainability scientists demarcate areas of normative, epistemic and socio-political concern.

Based on these results, Chapter 4 explores the tensions that arise between the approach of sustainability scientists and societal efforts to articulate and pursue sustainability goals, addressing three sets of questions: (1) How does sustainability science address the normative commitments of the sustainability discourse? What are the implications for science and for societal understandings of sustainability? (2) What are the epistemic challenges posed by sustainability problems? How does sustainability science address these? (3) What are the barriers to and opportunities for linking knowledge with action for sustainability? How does sustainability science as a field address these issues? The purpose of this analysis is to illuminate these often hidden tensions so that future research efforts in sustainability science might navigate them more effectively and contribute to positive social outcomes.

Based on the empirical and conceptual work done in Part I, Part II maps out an alternative, or perhaps complementary, pathway for sustainability science. Chapter 5 marks a shift from the empirical exploration of sustainability science to this conceptual project. It examines the epistemic and normative limitations of scientific approaches to sustainability in order to open the pathway for a framework centered on the articulation and pursuit of shared visions of social and natural well-being.

Chapter 6 borrows from the work of Nobel Laureate Herbert Simon and repositions sustainability science as a 'science of design' – that is, a normative science of what *ought* to be in order to achieve certain goals – rather than a science of what *is*. It will develop a foundation for a sustainability science that is solutions-oriented – one that aims to enrich public reasoning and deliberation while also working to generate social and technological innovations for a more sustainable future. This chapter then develops a set of design imperatives for sustainability science that aim to overcome the limitations of other approaches and focus research on the generation of positive, more sustainable, social outcomes. A sustainability science of design requires thinking beyond the current state of affairs to explore how preferred, more sustainable, futures can be developed and pursued. This requires that we rethink research priorities, the role of science in society and the training of the next generation of sustainability scientists.

Finally, Chapter 7 concludes with a discussion of the implications of a design science for sustainability, for how we organize research agendas, knowledge-producing organizations and the relationship between science and society. As environmental philosopher Dale Jamieson (1998: 191) aptly notes, '[w]hat is needed are simple and compelling stories that show us how to practically participate in creating the future in our daily lives, and how to engage in ongoing dialogue with others about how our everyday actions help to produce global realities.' Science alone cannot *make* a future happen; yet, it can help us identify the potential implications of such futures and their plausibility. As various research agendas for sustainability continue to emerge and develop, this project offers an opportunity to consider how science is informing and shaping societal efforts to pursue sustainability and an avenue for a more broadly reflexive and deliberative research program for sustainability regarding how knowledge is appropriated and the public purposes it serves.

Notes

1   Rittel and Weber (1973) identify ten distinguishing characteristics of wicked problems: (1) There is no definitive formulation of a wicked problem; (2) wicked problems have no stopping rule; (3) solutions to wicked problems are not true-or-false, but good-or-bad; (4) there is no immediate and no ultimate test of a solution to a wicked problem; (5) every solution of a wicked problem is a 'one-shot operation'; (6) wicked problems do not have enumerable (or an exhaustively describable) set of potential solutions; (7) every wicked problem is essentially unique; (8) every wicked problem can be considered to be a symptom of another problem; (9) the existence of a discrepancy representing a wicked problem can be explained in numerous ways; the choice of explanation determines the nature of the problem's resolution; and (10) the planner has no right to be wrong.

2   Of course, such problems are *still* wicked in many parts of the world. In large part the contextual variability of problems and the differential presence of technology, know-

how and the institutions necessary to regulate or deal with such problems can determine whether a problem is wicked or not. Whether a problem is tame or wicked is contextual.

References

Allenby, B.R., and D. Sarewitz. 2011. *The techno-human condition*. Cambridge, MA: MIT Press.

Brito L., and M.S. Smith. 2012. The state of the planet declaration. Planet Under Pressure Conference, London, UK. Available at: www.planetunderpressure2012.net/pdf/state_of_planet_declaration.pdf. [Accessed 24 May 2012.]

Carpenter, S.R., H.A. Mooney, J. Agard, D. Capistrano, R.S. DeFries, S. Diaz, T. Dietz, A.K. Duraiappah, A. Oteng-Yeboah, H.M. Pereira, C. Perrings, W.V. Reid, J. Sarukhan, R.J. Scholes, and A. Whyte. 2009. Science for managing ecosystem services: Beyond the Millennium Ecosystem Assessment. *Proceedings of the National Academy of Sciences* 106(5): 1305–12.

Cash, D.W., W.C. Clark, F. Alcock, N.M. Dickson, N. Eckley, D.H. Guston, J. Jäger, and R.B. Mitchell. 2003. Knowledge systems for sustainable development. *Proceedings of the National Academy of Sciences of the United States of America* 100(14): 8086–91.

Clark, W.C. 2007. Sustainability science: A room of its own. *Proceedings of the National Academy of Sciences* 104(6): 1737–8.

Clark, W.C., and N.M. Dickson. 2003. Sustainability science: The emerging research program. *Proceedings of the National Academy of Sciences of the United States of America* 100(14): 8059–61

Crow, M.M. 2007. None dare call it hubris: The limits of knowledge. *Issues in Science and Technology* Winter, 1–4.

Fischer, F. 2000. *Citizens, experts and the environment*. Durham, NC: Duke University Press.

Funtowicz, S.O., and J.R. Ravetz. 1993. Science for the post-normal age. *Futures* (257): 739–55.

Future Earth. 2013. *Future earth*. Available at: www.icsu.org/future-earth. [Accessed 24 July 2014.]

Gieryn, T.F. 1981. The aging of a science and its exploitation of innovation: Lessons from X-ray and radio astronomy. *Scientometrics*, 3(4): 325–34.

Gieryn, T.F. 1983. Boundary-work and the demarcation of science from non-science: Trains and interests in professional interests of scientists. *American Sociological Review* 48: 781–95.

Gieryn, T.F. 1995. Boundaries of science. In Sheila Jasanoff, Gerald E. Markle, James C. Petersen, and Trevor Pinch, (eds), rev. edn, *Handbook of science and technology studies*. Thousand Oaks, CA: Sage Publications.

Hoppe, R., and A. Peterse. 1993. *Handling frozen fire*. Boulder, CO: Westview Press.

Jamieson, D. 1998. Sustainability and beyond. *Ecological Economics* 24: 183–92.

Jasanoff, S. 2004. Ordering knowledge, ordering society. In Sheila Jasanoff, (ed.), *States of knowledge: The co-production of science and social order*, pp 13–45. New York: Routledge.

Jasanoff, S. 2005. *Designs on nature: Science and democracy in Europe and the United States*. Princeton, NJ: Princeton University Press

Jasanoff, S. 2010. Testing time for climate science. *Science* 328(5979): 695–6.

Kates, R.W., W.C. Clark, R. Corell, J.M. Hall, C.C. Jaeger, I. Lowe, J.J. McCarthy, H.J. Schellnhuber, B. Bolin, N.M. Dickson, S. Faucheux, G.C. Gallopín, A. Grübler, B. Huntley, J. Jäger, N.S. Jodha, R.E. Kasperson, A. Mabogunje, P. Matson, H. Mooney, B. Moore III, T. O'Riordan, and U. Svedin. 2001. Sustainability science. *Science* 292(5517): 641–2.

Latour, B. 1988. The politics of explanation: An alternative. *Knowledge and reflexivity: New frontiers in the sociology of knowledge*, 155–76.

Latour, B. 1993. *We have never been modern*. Cambridge, MA: Harvard University Press.

Latour, B. 2004. *Politics of nature: How to bring the sciences into democracy*. Cambridge, MA: Harvard University Press.

Levin, S.A., and W.C. Clark. 2010. *Toward a science of sustainability*. Report from Toward a science of sustainability Conference, Airlie Center, Warrenton, VA, 29 November–2 December 2009.

Lindblom, C. 1959. The science of muddling through. *Public Administration Review* 19(2): 79–88.

Lubchenco, J. 1998. Entering the century of the environment: A new social contract for science. *Science* 279(5350): 491.

Melosi, M.V. 2008. *The sanitary city: Environmental services in urban America from colonial times to the present*, abridged edn. Pittsburgh, PA: University of Pittsburgh Press.

Miller, T.R., B.A. Minteer, and L.C. Malan. 2011. The new conservation debate: The view from practical ethics. *Biological Conservation* 144: 948–57.

Miller, T.R., T.A. Muñoz-Erickson, and C.L. Redman. 2011. Transforming knowledge for sustainability: Fostering adaptability in academic institutions. *International Journal for Sustainability in Higher Education* 12(2): 177–92.

National Research Council. 1999. *Our common journey. A transition toward sustainability*. Washington, DC: National Academy Press.

Nelson, R.R. 1977. *The moon and the ghetto: An essay on public policy analysis*. The Fels Lectures on Public Policy Analysis. New York: W.W. Norton & Company.

Norton, B.G. 2005. *Sustainability. A philosophy of adaptive ecosystem management*. Chicago: University of Chicago Press.

Nowotny, H., P. Scott, and M. Gibbons. 2001. *Re-thinking science: Knowledge and the public in an age of uncertainty*. London: Polity Press.

Palmer, M., E. Bernhardt, E. Chornesky, S. Collins, A. Dobson, C. Duke, B. Gold, R. Jacobson, S. Kingsland, R. Kranz, M. Mappin, M.L. Martinez, F. Micheli, J. Morse, M.Pace, M. Pascual, S. Palumbi, O.J. Reichman, A. Simons, A. Townsend, M. Turner. 2005. Ecological science and sustainability for the 21st century. *Frontiers in Ecology and the Environment* 3(1): 4–11.

Reid, W.V., D. Chen, L. Goldfarb, H. Hackman, Y.T. Lee, K. Mokhele, E. Ostrom, K. Raivio, J. Rockström, H.J. Schellnhuber, and A. Whyte. 2010. Earth system science for global sustainability: Grand challenges. *Science* 330: 916–17.

Rittel, H.W.J., and M.M. Webber. 1973. Dilemmas in a general theory of planning. *Policy Sciences* 4: 155–69.

Sarewitz, D. 2004. How science makes environmental controversies worse. *Environmental Science & Policy* 7(5): 385–403.

Sarewitz, D., and R.R. Nelson. 2008. Progress in know-how: Its origins and limits. *innovations*, 3(1), 101–17.

Scott, J.C. 1998. *Seeing like a state: How certain schemes to improve the human condition have failed*. New Haven, CT: Yale University Press.

Shapin, S. and S. Schaffer. 1985. *Leviathan and the air-pump: Hobbes, Boyle, and the experimental life*. Princeton, NJ: Princeton University Press.

Stirling, A. 2008. 'Opening up' and 'closing down' power, participation, and pluralism in the social appraisal of technology. *Science, Technology & Human Values*, 33(2): 262–94.

Thompson, P.B. 2010. *The agrarian vision: Sustainability and environmental ethics*. Lexington, KY: University of Kentucky Press.

Turner, B.L. II, Pamela A. Matson, James J. McCarthy, Robert W. Corell, Lindsey Christensen,

Noelle Eckley, Grete K. Hovelsrud-Broda, Jeanne X. Kasperson, Roger E. Kasperson, Amy Luers, Marybeth L. Martello, Svein Mathiesen, Rosamond Naylor, Colin Polsky, Alexander Pulsipher, Andrew Schiller, Henrik Selin, and Nicholas Tyler. 2003a. Illustrating the coupled human – environment system for vulnerability analysis: Three case studies. *Proceedings of the National Academy of Sciences* 100(14): 8080–5.

Turner, B.L. II, Roger E. Kasperson, Pamela A. Matson, James J. McCarthy, Robert W. Corell, Lindsey Christensen, Noelle Eckley, Jeanne X. Kasperson, Amy Luers, Marybeth L. Martello, Colin Polsky, Alexander Pulsipher, and Andrew Schiller. 2003b. A framework for vulnerability analysis in sustainability science. *Proceedings of the National Academy of Sciences* 100(14): 8074–9.

2

A SCIENCE FOR SUSTAINABILITY

First coined in 1982 at the International Union for the Conservation of Nature (IUCN) World Parks Congress in Bali, the term 'sustainable development' was an attempt by conservation biologists and practitioners to integrate the goals of conservation with human and economic development, particularly in the developing world. Science, and more specifically the then emerging field of conservation biology, was viewed as crucial to revealing the societal and environmental benefits of conservation and providing knowledge to assist in the management of protected areas (Hughes-Evans and Aldrich 1983).

Emerging from conservation biology, a self-proclaimed 'mission–oriented' science (Soulé 1985), the framing of sustainable development was clearly normative. Sustainable development was an attempt to resolve the conflict between biodiversity conservation and human development. 'The ultimate choice,' stated Peter Thacher, Deputy Executive Director of the United Nations Environment Program, in his keynote address at the IUCN Congress, 'is between conservation or conflict. Trees now or tanks later. The choice for governments is either to find the means by which to pay now to stop the destruction of the natural resource base, or to be prepared to pay later, possibly in blood.' From the start, the power behind the argument for sustainable development was the ability to link empirical and normative claims (Miller *et al.* 2011). In this case, conservation biology aims to produce knowledge that provides the empirical evidence for the benefits of conservation and how it should be managed. As Miller *et al.* (2011) show, normative arguments about what *ought* to be conserved and how humans *should* interact with protected areas are inextricably intertwined with empirical claims regarding human well-being and biodiversity.

While the concept of sustainable development can be traced back further to the 1980 World Conservation Strategy and the 1972 Stockholm Conference on the Human Environment, it gained wide recognition and political cachet with the

1987 landmark publication by the World Commission on Economic Development (WCED) of *Our Common Future*, or, as it is more commonly known, the Brundtland Report. Bearing the name of the chair of the commission, Gro Harlem Brundtland, the Report famously defined sustainable development as 'development that meets the needs of the present without compromising the ability of future generations to meet their own needs' (WCED 1987: 43). While it made clear the importance of the role of technology, social organization and political action,[1] it relied heavily on and carved out a significant role for science in the pursuit of sustainable development. The Brundtland Report framed sustainable development as something that would be made possible by the power of global ecology to inform society's decisions and strategies (Jasanoff 1996). Jasanoff (1996: 185–6) continues, arguing that the Brundtland Report's idea of sustainable development and '…the indefinite survival of the human species could be assured through a universally acceptable marriage between scientific knowledge and rational stewardship.'

By the turn of the century, the 1999 report by the Board on Sustainable Development of the the US National Research Council (NRC), *Our Common Journey*, reviewed the status of the knowledge and know-how needed to embark on a sustainability transition. The Board defines a sustainability transition as occurring over the next two generations that 'should be able to meet the needs of a much larger but stabilizing human population, to sustain the life support systems of the planet, and to substantially reduce hunger and poverty' (NRC 1999: 31). The authors of the report, a group of geographers and ecologists with Robert Kates, William C. Clark and Pamela Matson emerging as leaders, argue that this transition is possible only with '*significant advances in basic knowledge*, in social capacity and technological capabilities to use it, and political will to turn this… into action' (NRC 1999, 7; emphasis added). It is in this context that the field of sustainability science is emerging.

The NRC report proposed the development of a 'sustainability science' that is place-based and problem-driven, integrating knowledge from different disciplines, across geographical and temporal scales, and between scholarship and practice. The concept began to gain traction in academic circles with the publication of 'Sustainability science' in *Science*. This article defined sustainability science as a new field that seeks 'to understand the fundamental character of interactions between nature and society' and enhance 'society's capacity to guide those interactions along more sustainable trajectories' (Kates *et al.* 2001, 641). Kates *et al.* (2001) and others (Cash *et al.* 2003; Matson 2009; NRC 1999) are quick to point to the normative reasons why such a research agenda is important – meeting human needs, especially for those living in poverty, while preserving the Earth's life support systems for future generations – and emphasize the necessity of linking knowledge to social action.

While it is a broad and evolving field at this point, several characteristics identify sustainability science, including fundamental research with a place-based focus on coupled human – natural systems from an interdisciplinary, problem-driven perspective (Cash *et al.* 2003; Clark and Dickson 2003; Kumazawa *et al.* 2009).

Turner *et al.* (2003a), for example, apply a vulnerability framework to the analysis of three coupled human-environment systems case studies including the Southern Yucatán peninsular region surrounding the Calakmul Biosphere Reserve.[2] The authors view vulnerability as residing 'in the condition and operation of the coupled human – environment system, including the response capacities and system feedbacks to the hazards encountered' (Turner *et al.* 2003a: 8080).

Another example of coupled systems research in sustainability is the work of Matson and colleagues on the Yaqui Valley in Sonora, Mexico. Matson *et al.* (2005) examine a system in which they seek to understand transitions under way as a result of population growth, urbanization, land use change and changes in the region's water regime. In these and other studies, sustainability science is being defined as an interdisciplinary field that seeks to understand the coupled human – environment dynamics underlying many pressing environmental problems (Carpenter *et al.* 2009; Ostrom 2007; Turner *et al.* 2003a).

As the research agendas for sustainability have developed so too have the programmatic elements of a growing scientific field including the establishment of research and education institutions and dedicated academic journals. Much of the activity in institutionalizing sustainability science has been centered around the American Association for the Advancement of Science (AAAS) Forum on Science and Technology for Sustainability, the Roundtable on Science and Technology for Sustainability Program at the National Academy of Sciences, and the Initiative on Science and Technology for Sustainability sponsored by the International Council of Science. Research and education programs and centers are also rapidly emerging. These include, but are certainly not limited to, the Global Institute of Sustainability and School of Sustainability at Arizona State University, the Center for Interactive Research on Sustainability at the University of British Columbia, Sustainability Studies at Lund University (Sweden), the Sustainability Science Program in the Center for International Development at Harvard University, and the Graduate Program in Sustainability Science at the University of Tokyo. Several academic journals have emerged including the *Proceedings of the National Academy of Sciences* Sustainability Science section, *Sustainability Science*, *Current Opinion in Environmental Sustainability*, and *Sustainability: Science, Policy and Practice*.

Use-inspired science

A critical motivating theme in sustainability science is that it is use-inspired, concerned with linking knowledge to action. Clark (2007) marked an important point in the development of the field with the establishment of a section devoted to sustainability science in the *Proceedings of the National Academy of Sciences*. In an editorial introducing the section, Clark (2007: 1737) characterizes sustainability science as a field similar to health science or agricultural science – 'a field defined by the problems it addresses rather than by the disciplines it employs.' Sustainability science, argues Clark, is use-inspired (as opposed to applied science or basic research) and seeks to facilitate a transition toward sustainability.

Clark's classification of sustainability science as use-inspired refers directly to science policy scholar and political scientist Donald Stokes's *Pasteur's Quadrant* (1997). Stokes reviews what he argues is a false dichotomy between basic and applied research. Basic research has been set up as the only 'pure' type of scientific research, aimed at revealing the fundamental laws of nature. Applied research, on the other hand, has been characterized as a more practical effort, engaged in solving problems as opposed to generating fundamental understanding. The physicist Niels Bohr and the inventor Thomas Edison are presented as examples of basic and applied research, respectively. This dichotomy has driven US science policy in the post-WWII era and continues to motivate perspectives on what counts as 'good' science.

Stokes contends that this two-dimensional image of science, which pits considerations of use against a quest for fundamental understanding, misses a critical category of scientific research – that is, use-inspired basic research. Use-inspired basic research 'seeks to extend the frontiers of understanding but is also inspired by considerations of use' (Stokes 1997: 74). Stokes illustrates his argument with the case of French chemist and microbiologist Louis Pasteur. Pasteur's work on vaccinations, pasteurization, fermentation and bacteria was motivated by a quest to *understand* microbiological processes and to *control* these processes for human use and benefit. Therefore, Stokes argues that Pasteur does not fit neatly into the traditional model of basic and applied research. Instead, a quadrant model of scientific research (Figure 2.1) is developed that accounts for use-inspired basic research, or 'Pasteur's Quadrant.' This is where Clark (2007) explicitly positions sustainability science.

Sustainability science is not unique, of course, among contemporary research efforts that aim to find a way to contribute directly to positive social and environmental outcomes while advancing fundamental understanding. For example, while

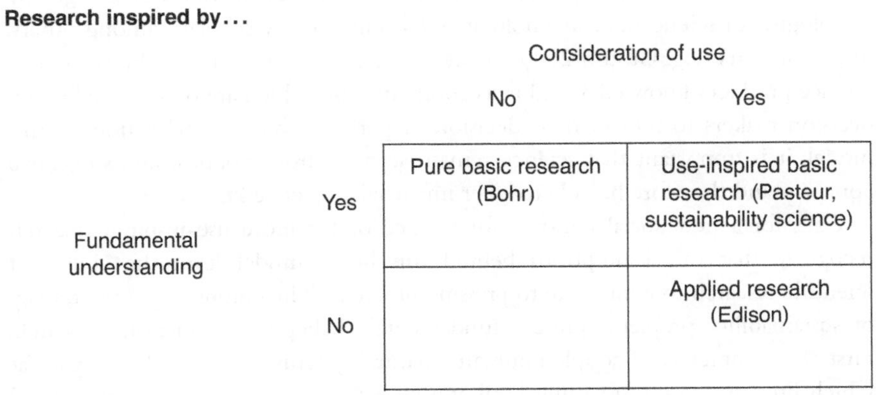

Research inspired by...

		Consideration of use	
		No	Yes
Fundamental understanding	Yes	Pure basic research (Bohr)	Use-inspired basic research (Pasteur, sustainability science)
	No		Applied research (Edison)

FIGURE 2.1 Quadrant model of scientific research.

Note: This model, adapted from Stokes (1997) and Clark (2007), depicts how sustainability scientists view the position of their field – pursuing questions that contribute to the fundamental understanding of human – environment interactions while also contributing to an ability to make decisions that contribute to more sustainable outcomes.

serving as President of the AAAS, Jane Lubchenco (1998) called for a new social contract for science. She argues that science has brought incalculable benefits to society while seeking knowledge that is largely divorced from considerations of societal benefit. However, society now faces a set of challenges that require scientists to shift their research priorities and translate knowledge to policy makers and the public more effectively. Scientists must address the most urgent needs of society, communicate the knowledge they produce to inform policy and management decisions and exercise good judgment in doing so. Similarly, Palmer *et al.* (2004, 2005) lay the foundations for a new pathway for ecological science – an 'ecology for a crowded planet.' The authors argue that for too long ecological research has focused on pristine ecosystems in which humans are viewed as a disturbance. They see a key role for ecology in informing decisions that support environmental sustainability and argue that a new research agenda must be built that focuses on ecosystem services and ecological design and restoration. More recently, Palmer (2012) has called for more 'actionable science' that serves society.

Lubchenco, Palmer and others (Gibbons 1999) contend that it is time for a new social contract for science. The 'old' social contract implicit in these arguments is that established by Vannevar Bush. In *Science—The Endless Frontier* (1945), Bush laid the foundation for the post-WWII relationship between science and society in the United States. Bush and other scientists (Polanyi 1962) argued that science delivers benefits to society most effectively and efficiently when scientists are able to act independently of political interference and pursue knowledge out of their own curiosity (Miller and Neff 2013). This relationship between scientific knowledge and its application is captured by the 1893 Chicago World's Fair unofficial motto – 'Science Finds, Industry Applies, Man Conforms.' This deterministic take on science and technology, or what some have referred to as the 'loading dock' or linear model of science and policy (see Figure 2.2),[3] has been widely challenged by sociologists of science and technology and science policy scholars, among others, in recent years (e.g. Guston 2000; Pielke 2007; Stokes 1997). In the linear model, science produces knowledge and facts about an issue, which are then picked up by decision makers to inform their decision or perhaps even compel action. In this model, it is important that science remain separate from political and subjective concerns and therefore be able to offer impartial, objective knowledge.

Calls for a new social contract for science or for more use-inspired research recognize that the assumptions behind this linear model limit the ability of scientific research to contribute to pressing problems. The complexity and urgency of sustainability problems present fundamental challenges to scientific research. First, the complexity of coupled human – natural systems and the scale and pace at which humans are transforming local and global ecologies cannot be understood through inquiries from single disciplines. This is a fundamental, epistemic challenge in how scientific research, disciplines and organizations are structured. Second, proponents argue that use-inspired basic research is required to meet the urgency of sustainability problems. Extraordinary circumstances – WWII, global environmental degradation – require extraordinary efforts. Such circumstances are so

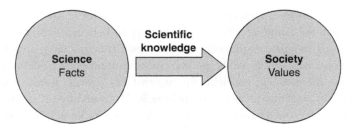

FIGURE 2.2 The 'loading dock' or linear model of science and decision-making.
Note: Adapted from Jasanoff and Wynne 1998: 8.

serious and time-sensitive that scientists must focus their research on issues of immediate concern to society and enhance their efforts to communicate knowledge to policy makers and the broader public.

How different scientific communities respond to these challenges and how effective those responses are – in terms both of producing positive social outcomes and of generating fundamental knowledge about our world – will provide insights into the power and/or limits of knowledge and serve as experiments for how scientific research can contribute to beneficial outcomes. Sustainability science, explicitly branded as problem-driven and use-inspired, is a case study for the exploration of how scientific fields and disciplines are reorganizing in the face of urgent and complex sustainability problems. As such, this work builds on Stokes and other science policy scholars (Guston 1999), in examining how scientific knowledge is perceived (in this case by sustainability scientists) to generate new understandings and contribute to better decisions relative to sustainability issues. This research, then, is partly an examination of what environmental philosopher, Paul Thompson, refers to as the paradox of sustainability, which 'arises because substantive, research-based approaches to sustainability may be too complex to effectively motivate appropriate social responses, especially in a culture where science is presumed to be value-free' (2010: 235). Before exploring the state of sustainability science in more detail in the following chapter, I now turn to a discussion of the theoretical and methodological framework offered by science and technology studies (STS) that I will be drawing from.

Science, technology and society

Though criticized as inoperable, overly ambiguous or simply promoting the status quo (Jamieson 1998; Marcuse 1998; Mebratu 1998; Worster 1994), sustainability might also be viewed as an effort to represent and articulate visions of social and natural well-being. Any effort by society to progress towards such a vision(s) will be an intensely social and political process. As scientists move to conduct research relevant to sustainability, they, in part, define sustainability – both in the production of knowledge and in the institutional structures of the field. This is not a process free of value choices or socio-political implications. Latour (2004: 95), for instance, cautions that 'the tempting aspect of the distinction between facts and values lies in its seeming modesty, its innocence, even: scientists define facts, only facts: they leave to politicians and moralists the even more daunting task of defining values.' In selecting theories and problems for sustainability science, scientists shape the concept of sustainability in society more broadly. Motivated by a desire to produce useful knowledge and a belief that access to the necessary knowledge will result in better decisions as well as a need to seek out the latest sources of funding, scientists often pursue research priorities that respond to pressing problems. The ways in which scientists construct research agendas for sustainability science and grapple with the deeply social, political and normative dimensions of both characterizing and pursuing sustainability have implications for the capacity of the field to provide useful knowledge and for how sustainability is constituted in society.

At the core of the STS research agenda has been the study of how the content of scientific and technical knowledge are constructed (Hacking 1999; Knorr-Cetina 1999; Latour 1988; Pinch and Bijker 1987; Vaughn 1996). Constructivism involves examining the social and political processes that influence and actively produce scientific and technological knowledge (Hacking 1999; Sismondo 2008). As Sismondo (2008: 13) notes, 'the history of STS is in part a history of increasing scope – starting with scientific knowledge, and expanding to artifacts, methods, materials, observations, phenomena, classifications, institutions, interests, histories, and cultures.' Following this, STS scholars have science and society co-produce one another. That is, science not only produces beliefs about how the world is, but also how it *ought* to be (Jasanoff 2004a; Latour 1993). As scientists describe social or ecological dynamics, they influence beliefs about what dynamics are sustainable – what society *ought* to do in order to be sustainable. Scientists may attempt to respond to the societal discourse on sustainability by researching problems identified by society as important. How sustainability science influences the social, political and normative dimensions of sustainability may render the concept of sustainability and the problems it encapsulates more or less tractable in terms of social action. STS scholars are well positioned to offer an analysis of both the boundary work being done to shape sustainability science and its relationship to society.

The concept of boundary work is particularly useful in this context for two reasons. First, boundary work allows for an examination of how the social, political and normative dimensions of sustainability are understood, articulated, bounded and settled by sustainability scientists. Gieryn (1999: 4) defines boundary work as 'the discursive attribution of selected qualities to scientists, scientific methods, and scientific claims for the purpose of drawing a rhetorical boundary between science and some less authoritative residual non-science.' For the purpose of this analysis, the concern is not on boundary work as the expulsion of rival authorities. Rather, the focus is on the construction of epistemic authority through scientific discourse and knowledge and how sustainability scientists deploy this authority to control discussions of research goals and demarcate social, political and normative discussions as either settled or beyond the scope of their claim-making territory. As

Gieryn (1999) argues, boundaries between science and non-science are constantly drawn and redrawn, allocating the epistemic authority of science and demarcating it from non-science.

Science and technology have been positioned as critical to society's ability to move towards sustainability. So too has science been shaped by the problems and concerns associated with sustainability as ecologists, geographers, environmental scientists and others move to conduct applied and use-inspired research (Lubchenco 1998; Stokes 1997; Palmer *et al.* 2004). Science, in other words, shapes and is shaped by sustainability problems and values. They co-produce one another (Jasanoff 2004b, 2005; Latour 1993) – 'the products of the sciences, both cognitive and material, embody beliefs not only about how the world *is*, but also how it *ought* to be. Natural and social orders... are produced at one and the same time' (Jasanoff 2005: 19). As philosopher of science Helen Longino (1990) notes, the object of inquiry is not just nature, but nature under a specific description – teleological, mechanistic or a complex adaptive system, for example. Before any knowledge is produced or research performed, the subject matter or system of inquiry must be characterized 'in ways that make certain kinds of explanation appropriate and others inappropriate' (Longino 1990). Scientific communities do not want just knowledge, but knowledge about a particular set of things (Longino 2002). Concealing the reliance of scientific inquiry on background assumptions and values discourages the investigation of alternative frameworks and stymies the development of new insights and knowledge (Longino 1990). Human – environment interactions underlying (un)sustainable dynamics and the broad normative agenda of sustainability are sufficiently complex and diverse to allow for a variety of interpretations, or constructions, of sustainability. Utilizing boundary work and co-production as conceptual tools, this book will uncover these background assumptions as they are taking shape in emerging sustainability science communities and, in Part II, it will turn to an exploration of alternative pathways for sustainability science.

As sustainability scientists move to conduct research relevant to sustainability, they, in part, define it. In selecting theories and problems for sustainability science, scientists shape the concept of sustainability in society more broadly. Motivated by a desire to produce useful knowledge and a belief that access to the necessary knowledge will result in better decisions (Bocking 2004; Kinzig 2001; Lubchenco 1998; Palmer *et al.* 2005; Raven 2002) as well as a need to seek out the latest sources of funding (Braun 1998), scientists often pursue research priorities that respond to pressing problems (Miller and Neff 2013). The ways in which scientists construct research agenda(s) for sustainability science have implications both for the capacity of the field to provide useful knowledge and for how sustainability is constituted in society. STS is well positioned to offer an analysis of this co-production as well as of how boundary work is shaping sustainability science and its relationship to society. In the following chapter, I will trace the normative, epistemic and socio-political boundaries that are being drawn in sustainability science in order both to understand these assumptions, examining potential tensions and limitations, and to explore the potential for STS to contribute to a reconstruction of sustainability science. Here, I will discuss the shift to reconstruction; but, first, I turn to a brief description of the methodological approach taken to analyze sustainability science.

Methodological approach

The methodological approach follows the pioneering study of conservation biologists and biodiversity by Takacs (1996). Through interviews with leading figures in conservation, Takacs examines how they have shaped and promoted the concept of biodiversity, including its normative character. In a similar fashion, the analysis in this book provides a rich description of emerging research agendas in sustainability science and how scientists envision the knowledge produced by the field contributing to society.

In-depth interviews were conducted with 28 key researchers in sustainability science between June 2009 and January 2010. Interview subjects were identified through their involvement in critical developments in the sustainability science literature, through association with sustainability research programs and by key informants. Interview subjects were drawn from the USA, the Netherlands, Sweden, the UK, Japan and Canada. Several researchers that are outside of the mainstream sustainability science community were interviewed in order to get alternative perspectives on this developing research area. Interviews began with several preset questions and topics but allowed for flexibility around the research interests and perspective of the interview subject. Interviews were conducted in person when possible and over the telephone in select cases. Interviews were conducted in English and lasted from 45 minutes to 1.5 hours in length.[4]

In addition to the interviews, a literature review and content analysis of the leading journals, reports and papers in the field was performed. Journals analyzed included the *Proceedings of the National Academy of Sciences, Science, Nature, Sustainability: Science, Policy and Practice, Sustainability Science* and *Current Opinion in Environmental Sustainability*, as well as select papers in other journals. Activities sponsored by the AAAS, the National Academy of Sciences and the National Science Foundation have been critical in establishing a research agenda for the field. Workshop reports and other outcomes from these activities were analyzed as well.

Content analysis of the literature was coded to focus on the normative, epistemic and socio-political claims of sustainability science. Journal articles and workshop reports, however, do not always provide the detail necessary to explore the motivations behind research agendas. Interviews, then, were important sources of data to examine the normative dimensions of this emerging field and its social and political context. This qualitative, mixed methodological approach enables a 'thick' description of emerging visions of sustainability science; that is, an approach that steers away from descriptive cataloguing of, in this case, the culture of a scientific field, and instead seeks the 'connections and general patterns that are characteristic of a certain context' (Adger *et al.* 2003: 195; Geertz 1973).

Reflexivity and reconstruction in STS

As noted earlier, STS scholarship has focused on the construction of scientific knowledge and boundaries between science and decision making or science and society. While such analyses are necessary and fruitful, they can limit the ability of STS scholarship to actively contribute to the exploration and development of alternative research trajectories and a more nuanced relationship between science and social context. In Part II, I follow STS scholars who have urged the field to move beyond constructivist analyses to propose potential *reconstructions* for sustainability science (Hess 2007; Woodhouse 2006; Woodhouse *et al.* 2002). This is part of a larger turn in STS toward an 'engaged program' (Sismondo 1998), exemplified by STS researchers engaging scientists, engineers, decision makers and the public (e.g. Fisher and Schuurbiers 2013; Barben *et al.* 2008; Tlili and Dawson 2010).

Woodhouse (2006), for example, describes how 'brown' chemistry came to have a privileged position over 'green' chemistry. Woodhouse notes that in its early stages, it was not obvious that 'brown' chemistry, or more toxin-intensive chemistry, would become dominant. Instead, 'brown' chemistry had several advantages including a better structural position, a quiescent public and habits of thought that led to it becoming the dominant paradigm. Woodhouse then lays out the reconstructivist agenda by asking how we might better understand the micro-local reality of scientific research agendas, reduce elite appropriation of knowledge and direct technical capabilities to more justifiable public purposes.

As research agendas for sustainability continue to develop (e.g. Clark and Dickson 2003; Gibson 2006; Mihelcic *et al.* 2003; Miller *et al.* 2013; Palmer *et al.* 2005), a reconstructivist approach offers an avenue for a more broadly reflexive and deliberative science and technology (S&T) research program. An STS analysis of sustainability science can inject a needed dose of reflexivity to the field. Reflexivity is a recursive process that focuses attention on how the object of study is represented by, in this case, scientists. In turn, it also draws attention to how attributes of the subject (e.g. epistemic and normative presuppositions) constitute representations of the object of study and how these very representations might condition the subject (Stirling 2006).

Reflexivity is particularly important in socially relevant areas like sustainability. As discussed earlier, science helps to shape our representations of what a sustainable or unsustainable system looks like. Given the complexity and contested nature of sustainability problems, awareness of how epistemic and normative assumptions shape representations and how, in turn, these representations shape potential actions and future research is critical to ensuring that sustainability science fosters discussion and debate over normative aims and appropriate action. An unreflexive sustainability science risks 'closing down' such debate and 'block boxing' normative and epistemic claims. Reflexivity requires a transparency and openness with regards to normative premises, epistemic claims and position, and an understanding of the limits of knowledge in terms of both what can be known and observed about a system and the variability of the role of knowledge in different socio-political contexts (Grunwald 2004; Miller *et al.* 2011). Reflexivity will be discussed further in Part II as a critical element of a reconstructed sustainability science.[5]

Like much of STS research (Fujimura 1996; Latour 1988; Jasanoff 2005; Knorr-Cetina 1999), the reconstructivist approach taken here works to uncover these issues. This is the focus of Part I. Where reconstruction moves beyond a traditional constructivist approach is in the active engagement with sustainability science to 'open up' (Stirling 2008) alternative research pathways, the meaning of sustainability and institutional configurations for research organization. This is done theoretically and conceptually here, in Part II, but also through an engagement in the sustainability science literature and community (cf. Miller 2013; Miller *et al.* 2014). This is partly an interdisciplinary gesture to reach across disciplinary divides. Importantly, it is also a normative position. As mentioned in the discussion of wicked problems in the previous chapter, sustainability encapsulates concerns about nature, the sense of place, culture and what options and opportunities we ought to keep open for future generations (Norton 2005). Sustainability is itself a boundary concept (Jasanoff 1990) with an interpretative flexibility that enables a plurality of potentially divergent views and values and a certain degree of normative ambiguity (Stirling 2006). STS scholarship has shown how S&T can shape and even close down discussion of such value-laden issues. Part I explores the various ways the sustainability science community is interpreting sustainability. The reconstructivist approach taken in Part II aims to inform a sustainability science that works to foster and open up these discussions.

Conclusion

Sustainability science provides an opportunity to explore how emerging fields are reorganizing to respond to pressing social and environmental problems and conduct use-inspired basic research. As such, this work informs STS examination of boundary work, particularly around value-laden and socio-politically relevant areas like sustainability. It also contributes to science policy studies and STS in exploring how scientists interpret public values (Bozeman 2007) and attempt to link scientific knowledge to those values. Building on and utilizing insights from STS, reconstruction helps to shape a sustainability science that supports deliberation on the normative goals of sustainability and links knowledge to beneficial outcomes. In the following chapter, I discuss the emerging visions of sustainability science and analyze how scientists are drawing boundaries around normative, epistemic and socio-political claims.

Notes

1   As well as defining sustainable development the authors note that, while it does imply limits, they are 'not absolute limits but limitations imposed by the present state of technology and social organization on environmental resources and by the ability of the biosphere to absorb the effects of human activities. But technology and social

organization can be both managed and improved to make way for a new era of economic growth' (WCED 1987: 8).

2 Vulnerability is defined as 'the degree to which a system, subsystem, or system component is likely to experience harm due to exposure to a hazard, either a perturbation or stress/stressor' (Turner *et al.* 2003b: 8074).

3 I am indebted to my friend and colleague, Kate Darby, and the IGERT in Urban Ecology group at Arizona State University for this label and for heated discussions about the linear model.

4 See Appendices A and B for a list of interview subjects and the interview protocol.

5 There is also a long history of reflexivity in the social sciences. For reviews of reflexivity in the social sciences as well as science studies, see Beck (1992), Bourdieu (2001), Giddens (1991), Hess (2011), Sismondo (2008).

References

Adger, W.N., S. Huq, K. Brown, D. Conway, and M. Hulme. 2003. Adaptation to climate change in the developing world. *Progress in development studies*, 3(3): 179–95.

Barben, D., E. Fisher, C. Selin, and D.H. Guston. 2008. 38 Anticipatory governance of nanotechnology: Foresight, engagement, and integration. In Edward J. Hackett, Olga Amsterdamska, Michael E. Lynch, and Judy Wajcman, (eds), *Handbook of Science and Technology Studies*. Cambridge, MA: MIT Press.

Beck, U. 1992. *The risk society. Towards a new modernity*. London: Sage.

Bocking, S. 2004. *Nature's experts: science, politics, and the environment*. New Brunswick, NJ: Rutgers University Press.

Bourdieu, P. 2001. *Masculine domination*. Palo Alto, CA: Stanford University Press.

Bozeman, Barry. 2007. *Public Values and Public Interest: Counterbalancing Economic Individualism*. Washington, DC: George Washington University Press.

Braun, D. 1998. The role of funding agencies in the cognitive development of science. *Research Policy* 27(8): 807–21.

Bush, V. 1945. *The endless frontier*. Washington, DC: National Science Foundation.

Carpenter, S.R., H.A. Mooney, J. Agard, D. Capistrano, R.S. DeFries, S. Diaz, T. Dietz, A.K. Duraiappah, A. Oteng-Yeboah, H.M. Pereira, C. Perrings, W.V. Reid, J. Sarukhan, R.J. Scholes, and A. Whyte. 2009. Science for managing ecosystem services: Beyond the Millennium Ecosystem Assessment. *Proceedings of the National Academy of Sciences* 106(5): 1305–12.

Cash, D.W., W.C. Clark, F. Alcock, N.M. Dickson, N. Eckley, D.H. Guston, J. Jäger, and R.B. Mitchell. 2003. Knowledge systems for sustainable development. *Proceedings of the National Academy of Sciences of the United States of America* 100(14) (July 8): 8086–91.

Clark, W.C. 2007. Sustainability science: A room of its own. *Proceedings of the National Academy of Sciences* 104(6): 1737–8.

Clark, W.C. and N.M. Dickson. 2003. Sustainability science: The emerging research program. *Proceedings of the National Academy of Sciences of the United States of America* 100(14) (July 8): 8059–61.

Fisher, E. and D. Schuurbiers 2013. Socio-technical integration research: Collaborative inquiry at the midstream of research and development. In *Early engagement and new technologies: Opening up the laboratory* (pp. 97–110). Dordrecht, Netherlands: Springer.

Fujimura, J.H. 1996. *Crafting science: A sociohistory of the quest for the genetics of cancer*. Cambridge, MA: Harvard University Press.

Geertz, C. 1973. *The interpretation of cultures*. New York: Basic Books.

Gibbons, M. 1999. Science's new social contract with society. *Nature* 402: C81.

Gibson, R.B. 2006. Sustainability assessment: Basic components of a practical approach. *Impact Assessment and Project Appraisal* 24(3): 170–82.

Giddens, A. 1991. *Modernity and self-identity: self and identity in the late modern age.* Cambridge: Polity.

Gieryn, T.F. 1983. 'Boundary-work and the demarcation of science from non-science: Trains and interests in professional interests of scientists. *American Sociological Review* 48: 781–95.

Gieryn, T.F. 1999. *Cultural boundaries of science. Credibility on the line.* Chicago: University of Chicago Press.

Grunwald, A. 2004. Strategic knowledge for sustainable development: The need for reflexivity and learning at the interface between science and society. *International Journal of Foresight and Innovation Policy* 1(1/2): 150.

Guston, D.H. 1999. Evaluating the first US consensus conference: the impact of the citizens' panel on telecommunications and the future of democracy. *Science, Technology and Human Values* 24(4): 451–82.

Guston, D.H. 2000. Retiring the social contract for science. *Issues in Science and Technology*, 16(4): 32–6.

Hacking, I. 1999. *The social construction of what?.* Cambridge, MA: Harvard University Press.

Hess, D.J. 2007. *Alternative pathways in science and industry: Activism, innovation, and the environment in an era of globalization.* Cambridge, MA: MIT Press.

Hess, D.J. 2011. Bourdieu and science studies: Toward a reflexive sociology. *Minerva*, 49(3): 333–48.

Hughes-Evans, D. and J.L. Aldrich. 1983. The role of the educator... to find not search. *The Environmentalist*, 3: 81–2.

Jamieson, D. 1998. Sustainability and beyond. *Ecological Economics* 24: 183–92

Jasanoff, S. 1990. *The fifth branch: Science advisers as policymakers.* Cambridge, MA: Harvard University Press.

Jasanoff, S. 1996. Science and norms in global environmental regimes. In Fen Osler Hampson and Judith Reppy, (eds), *Earthly Goods: Environmental Change and Social Justice*, pp 173–97. Ithaca, NY: Cornell University Press.

Jasanoff, S. 2004a. Afterward. In Sheila Jasanoff, (ed.), *States of knowledge: The co-production of science and social order*, pp 274–85. New York: Routledge.

Jasanoff, S. 2004b. Ordering knowledge, ordering society. In Sheila Jasanoff, (ed.), *States of knowledge: The co-production of science and social order*, pp 13–45. New York: Routledge

Jasanoff, S. 2005. *Designs on nature: Science and democracy in Europe and the United States.* Princeton, NJ: Princeton University Press.

Jasanoff, S. and B. Wynne. 1998. Science and decisionmaking. In Steve Rayner and Elizabeth Malone, (eds), *Human Choice and Climate Change, Vol. 1: The Societal Framework*, pp 1–87. Columbus, OH: Battelle Press.

Kates, R.W., W.C. Clark, R. Corell, J. Michael Hall, C.C. Jaeger, I. Lowe, J.J. McCarthy, H.J. Schellnhuber, B. Bolin, N.M. Dickson, S. Faucheux, G.C. Gallopin, A. Grübler, B. Huntley, J. Jäger, N.S. Jodha, R.E. Kasperson, A. Mabogunje, P. Matson, H. Mooney, B. Moore III, T. O'Riordan, and U. Svedin. 2001. Sustainability science. *Science* 292(5517): 641–2.

Kinzig, A P. 2001. Bridging disciplinary divides to address environmental and intellectual challenges. *Ecosystems* 4: 709–15.

Knorr-Cetina, K. 1999. *Epistemic cultures: How the sciences make knowledge.* Cambridge, MA: Harvard University Press.

Kumazawa, T., O. Saito, K. Kozaki, T. Matsui, and R. Mizoguchi. 2009. Toward knowledge structuring of sustainability science based on ontology engineering. *Sustainability Science* 4(2): 315.

Latour, B. 1988. The politics of explanation: an alternative. *Knowledge and reflexivity: New frontiers in the sociology of knowledge*, 155–76.

Latour, B. 1993. *We have never been modern*. Cambridge, MA: Harvard University Press.

Latour, B. 2004. *The politics of nature: How to bring the sciences into democracy*. Cambridge, MA: Harvard University Press.

Longino, H. 1990. *Science as social knowledge: Values and objectivity in scientific inquiry*. Princeton, NJ: Princeton University Press.

Longino, H. 2002. *The fate of knowledge*. Princeton, NJ: Princeton University Press.

Lubchenco, J. 1998. Entering the century of the environment: A new social contract for science. *Science* 279(5350): 491.

Marcuse, P. 1998. Sustainability is not enough. *Environment and Urbanization* 10(2): 103–11.

Matson, P. 2009. The sustainability transition. *Issues in Science and Technology* Summer 2009: 39–42.

Matson, P., A. Luers, K. Seto, R. Naylor, and I. Ortiz-Monasterio. 2005. People, land use and environment in the Yaqui Valley, Sonora, Mexico. In B. Entwisle and P. Stern, (eds), *Population, Land Use, and Environment*, pp 238–64. Washington, DC: National Research Council.

Mebratu, D. 1998. Sustainability and sustainable development: historical and conceptual review. *Environmental Impact Assessment Review* 18: 493–520.

Mihelcic, J.R., J.C. Crittenden, M.J. Small, D.R. Shonnard, D.R. Hokanson, Q. Zhang, H. Chen, S.A. Sorby, V.U. James, J.W. Sutherland, and J.L. Schnoor.. 2003. Sustainability science and engineering: The emergence of a new metadiscipline. *Environmental Science and Technology* 37(23): 5314–24.

Miller, T.R. 2013. Constructing sustainability science: Emerging perspectives and research trajectories. *Sustainability Science* 8(2): 279–93.

Miller, T.R., B.A. Minteer, and L.C. Malan. 2011. The new conservation debate: the view from practical ethics. *Biological Conservation* 144: 948–57.

Miller, T.R. and N.W. Neff. 2013. De-facto science policy in the making: How scientists shape science policy and why it matters (or, why STS and STP scholars should socialize). *Minerva*, 51(3): 295–315.

Miller, T.R., A. Wiek, D. Sarewitz, J. Robinson, L. Olsson, D. Kriebel, and D. Loorbach. 2014. The future of sustainability science: a solutions-oriented research agenda. *Sustainability Science*, 9(2): 239–46.

National Research Council. 1999. *Our common journey: A transition toward sustainability*. Washington, DC: National Academy Press.

Norton, B.G. 2005. *Sustainability. A philosophy of adaptive ecosystem management*. Chicago: University of Chicago Press.

Ostrom, E. 2007. A diagnostic approach for going beyond panaceas. *Proceedings of the National Academy of Sciences of the United States of America* 104(39): 15181–7.

Palmer, M.A. 2012. Socioenvironmental sustainability and actionable science. *BioScience*, 62(1): 5–6.

Palmer, M., E. Bernhardt, E. Chornesky, S. Collins, A. Dobson, C. Duke, B. Gold, R. Jacobson, S. Kingsland, R. Kranz, M. Mappin, M.L. Martinez, F. Micheli, J. Morse, M. Pace, M. Pascual, S. Palumbi, O.J. Reichman, A. Simons, A. Townsend, M. Turner. 2004. Ecology for a crowded planet. *Science* 304(5675): 1251–2.

Palmer, M., E. Bernhardt, E. Chornesky, S. Collins, A. Dobson, C. Duke, B. Gold, R. Jacobson, S. Kingsland, R. Kranz, M. Mappin, M.L. Martinez, F. Micheli, J. Morse, M. Pace, M. Pascual, S. Palumbi, O.J. Reichman, A. Simons, A. Townsend, M. Turner. 2005. Ecological science and sustainability for the 21st century. *Frontiers in Ecology and the Environment* 3(1): 4–11

Pielke, R.A. Jr 2007. *The honest broker: Making sense of science in policy and politics*. Cambridge: Cambridge University Press.

Pinch, T.J., and W.E. Bijker. 1987. The social construction of facts and artifacts: Or how the sociology of science and the sociology of technology might benefit each other. *The social construction of technological systems: New directions in the sociology and history of technology*, 17.

Polanyi, M. 1962. The republic of science: Its political and economic theory. *Minerva* 1: 54–74.

Raven, P.H. 2002. Science, sustainability and the human prospect. *Science* 297(5583): 954–8.

Sismondo, S. 1998. The mapping metaphor in philosophy of science. *Cogito* 12: 41–50.

Sismondo, S. 2008. Science and technology studies and an engaged program. *The handbook of science and technology studies*, 13–31.

Soulé, M. 1985. What is conservation biology? *BioScience* 35: 727–33.

Stirling, A. 2006. Precaution, foresight, and sustainability: Reflection and reflexivity in the governance of science and technology. In J.P.Voß, D. Bauknecht, R. Kemp, (eds), *Reflexive Governance for Sustainable Development*. Cheltenham, UK: Edward Elgar.

Stirling, A. 2008. 'Opening up' and 'closing down': Power, participation, and pluralism in the social appraisal of technology. *Science, Technology, and Human Values* 33(2): 262–94.

Stokes, D. 1997. *Pasteur's Quadrant: Basic Science and Technological Innovation*. Washington, DC: Brookings Institution Press.

Takacs, D. 1996. *The idea of biodiversity: Philosophies of paradise*. Baltimore, MD: Johns Hopkins University Press.

Thatcher, P., Former Deputy Executive Director of the UN Environment Programme, in a speech on worldwide deforestation, Bali World National Parks Conference, 1982.

Thompson, P.B. 2010. *The agrarian vision: Sustainability and environmental ethics*. Lexington, KY: University of Kentucky Press.

Tlili, A., and E. Dawson. 2010. Mediating science and society in the EU and UK: From information-transmission to deliberative democracy? *Minerva*, 48(4): 429–61.

Turner, B.L. II, A. Pamela, J.J. Matson, R.W. McCarthy, L.C. Corell, L. Christensen, N. Eckley, G.K. Hovelsrud-Broda, J.X. Kasperson, R.E. Kasperson, A. Luers, M.L. Martello, S. Mathiesen, R. Naylor, C. Polsky, A. Pulsipher, A. Schiller, H. Selin, and N. Tyler. 2003a. Illustrating the coupled human – environment system for vulnerability analysis: Three case studies. *Proceedings of the National Academy of Sciences* 100(14): 8080–5.

Turner, B.L. II, Roger E. Kasperson, Pamela A. Matson, James J. McCarthy, Robert W. Corell, Lindsey Christensen, Noelle Eckley, Jeanne X. Kasperson, Amy Luers, Marybeth L. Martello, Colin Polsky, Alexander Pulsipher, and Andrew Schiller. 2003b. A framework for vulnerability analysis in sustainability science. *Proceedings of the National Academy of Sciences* 100(14): 8074–9.

Vaughn, D. 1996. *The Challenger launch decision*. Chicago: University of Chicago Press.

Woodhouse, E., D. Hess, S. Breyman, and B. Martin. 2002. Science studies and activism possibilities and problems for reconstructivist agendas. *Social Studies of Science*, 32(2): 297–319.

Woodhouse, E.J. 2006. Nanoscience, green chemistry, and the privileged position of science. *The new political sociology of science: Institutions, networks, and power*, 148–81.

World Commission on Environment and Development (WCED). 1987. *Our common future*. New York: Oxford University Press.

Worster, D. 1994. Nature and the disorder of history. *Environmental History Review*, 18(2): 1–15.

3
CONSTRUCTING SUSTAINABILITY SCIENCE

Sustainability science, like much use-inspired research, explores a world that is inherently complex and uncertain. It tangles with deeply normative and contested questions about our relationship to nature, our consumption of natural resources and the value we place on the future. How, then, are sustainability scientists to navigate this complex terrain, drawing boundaries around appropriate research questions for the field, while both acknowledging the value-laden nature of sustainability questions and pursuing the scientific, value-free ideal?

This chapter[1] focuses on three core issues in the construction of sustainability science:

1. how sustainability scientists define and bound sustainability;
2. how and why various research agendas are being constructed to address these notions of sustainability; and
3. how scientists see their research contributing to societal efforts to move towards sustainability.

In particular, I will focus on the boundary work performed around the normative, epistemic and socio-political claims of sustainability scientists. Sustainability, as noted earlier, is a value-laden concept. How scientists interpret the normative dimensions of sustainability may influence the directions of the research agendas and shape the perceived credibility of alternative normative claims and concerns – from other scientists, decision makers or other stakeholders. The epistemic claims of sustainability scientists – or what knowledge they seek about what set of things – demarcate those areas worthy of pursuit by the field. How these claims balance the potential tension between basic research and use-inspired research will inform developments in use-inspired basic research as well as the reconstruction of sustainability undertaken in Part II. Finally, given the field's problem and use-inspired orientation, uncovering sustainability scientists' socio-political claims – that is, how knowledge will be useful and for what actions – is critical for understanding the field's situatedness and analyzing the ways in which scientists might be limiting the field or enabling it to contribute to social action for sustainability. These claims will be explored here and tensions between them will be discussed in Chapter 4.

The discussion in this chapter is informed by in-depth interviews conducted with 28 key researchers in sustainability science and an extensive review of the relevant literature. By revealing how scientists are bounding elements of the sustainability discourse and the relationship between knowledge and action, this chapter will lay the foundation for the reconstruction of sustainability science.

Normative claims: defining sustainability

In discussions on sustainability there is one question that is inevitably raised – 'What is sustainability?' Follow-up questions typically attempt to ask what is being sustained, for whom and for how long. The answers to such questions are anything but trivial and are value-laden, particularly in the context of sustainability science (Norton 2005). The interests scientists select, observes the German sociologist Ulrich Beck (1992: 174), 'on whom and what they project the causes, how they interpret the problems of society, what sort of potential solutions they bring into view – these are anything but neutral decisions.'

The purpose of examining scientists' definitions of sustainability is not to refute or endorse one or another. In fact, some of the scientists interviewed discussed and even endorsed multiple and sometimes conflicting definitions. Definitions of sustainability serve as an important point from which to analyze the normative claims of scientists and how they are demarcated from epistemic claims. Two primary themes emerged in discussions on the meaning of sustainability: *universalist sustainability* and *procedural sustainability*. Importantly, each of the definitions involves normative notions of sustainability, but with varying emphases and implications. How do scientists define sustainability? To what extent do scientists address these value-laden questions related to sustainability? How might this influence the way(s) by which society comes to define sustainability? How do they envision their research contributing to societal efforts to move toward sustainability? These are the questions that will be addressed in the following discussion.

Universalist sustainability

Many of the interview subjects and much of the literature reviewed refer to one of two definitions – those put forth by the WCED and the NRC report. Parris and Kates (2003: 8068), for example, define a transition to sustainability as 'stabilizing world population, meeting its needs and reducing poverty and hunger while maintaining the planet's life support systems.' Similarly, a report from the Third World Academy of Sciences (Hassan 2001: 70) defines sustainability as 'meeting current human needs while preserving the environment and natural resources needed by future generations.' Carl Folke of the Stockholm Resilience Centre sums up this perspective: 'How can we develop and continue to improve human well-being and our life as a species on [this] planet...? That's really what sustainability is about for me.' I refer to this set of definitions as *universalist (or thin) sustainability* – meeting human needs, both now and in the future, without degrading the planet's life support systems.

Political theorist Michael Walzer (1994) uses 'thin morality'[2] or 'moral minimalism' to describe concepts that encourage widespread agreement but do not substantively translate to the level of individual behavior changes or conflict with more contextual notions of what is moral or desirable. Walzer notes that virtually every human society can agree that the idea of justice is one worth pursuing; however, what justice looks like in various places or contexts can be very different and even conflict. This does not mean that thin or morally minimal descriptions of justice are meaningless or morally shallow. Instead, thin morality can assume a deeply compelling character, since it consists of moral notions on which all can agree. It is this universality that has allowed thin sustainability to gain traction in both science and society.

At the core of sustainability is a concern that current human activities and their effects on the environment are undercutting the ability of ecological systems to support the well-being of both current and future generations. 'Despite the awe in which we hold nature and the value we place on its conservation,' argues William C. Clark (2010: 82), co-Director of the Sustainability Science Program at Harvard University, 'ours is ultimately a project that seeks to understand what is, can be, and ought to be the human use of the earth.'

Thin sustainability serves as a general normative frame, or in the words of Jan Rotmans, former Director of the Dutch Research Institute for Transitions (DRIFT), a 'normative orientation,' for sustainability scientists. It is both a source of motivation and a normative goal for research. Sustainability scientists are able to tap into the moral underpinnings of sustainability to express concern over the impacts of human activity and justify research agendas. Moral minimalism 'is everyone's morality because it is no one's in particular; subjective interest and cultural expression have been avoided or cut away' (Walzer 1994: 7). So too is science perceived by many scientists and the public as universalist, objective and free of cultural context. A sustainability from which 'subjective interest and cultural expression have been avoided or cut away' serves to reinforce this image of science and maintain its authoritative role in society (Collingridge and Reeve 1986; Jasanoff 1987).

'Thick morality' or 'moral maximalism,' on the other hand, is contextual and embedded in a certain place or unique to a certain people. Maximalism 'is idiomatic, particularist, and circumstantial... [it] is the socially constructed idealism of *these* people' (Walzer 1994: 39). Norton (2005) picks up on this, arguing that sustainability has the potential for constructing an improved language for discussion of environmental problems because it is both descriptive and evaluative. In other words, sustainability is a 'thick' concept that can encapsulate a great deal of information and present that information in a way that makes explicit its importance to widely held social values. Scientists have embraced thin sustainability and its universality, potentially limiting the degree to which deeper discussions over a 'thick sustainability' and the role of science take place. As Jamieson (1995, 1998) notes, attempts to provide scientific or technical definitions for highly normative concepts, such as sustainability or ecosystem health, often result in a circumvention of ethical and political issues or lead to a bedeviled debate in which ethical, political and scientific issues are confused.

The values of sustainability motivate scientists but, at the same time, scientists are careful to control the degree to which such values infiltrate science. Parris and Kates (2003: 8068), for instance, believe that 'defining sustainability is ultimately a social choice about what to develop, what to sustain, and for how long.' Pam Matson of Stanford University, a leading figure in the field, separates the values of society from the values of the scientist:

> the values are the values of the decision makers. And, of course, scientists all have their own value systems, too. And mine would say – ...meeting the needs of people while protecting the life support systems of the planet. I'm including the ecosystems and the species within them, on land and in the oceans, because I think they provide all of the [ecosystem] services that we need.

Boundaries are drawn between personal values and those that might influence the way society and decision makers understand sustainability. The values and motivations of scientists and sustainability science are acknowledged, but at a level that is universal. It is 'everyone's morality because it is no one's in particular.' I refer to this boundary work as *normative distancing*. These are the scientists' values and they are everyone's values. Both the definition of sustainability and the usefulness of science to sustainability efforts are universal.

The context and conflict that come with thickness are absent in thin sustainability. 'With thickness,' notes Walzer (1994: 6), 'comes qualification, compromise, complexity, and disagreement.' Thomas Parris of ISciences, a sustainable science and information consulting group, and a member of the NRC's Board on Sustainable Development, notes that the selection of a thin definition of sustainability is often deliberate: 'It's the part that everyone can agree on... The point is that there's a core... because people don't universally agree to the various additional layers that people add on to it...' A universalist sustainability creates a normative distance between science and values that enables scientists to avoid opening up an arena in which the role of science and the knowledge produced by scientists may be contested along with other components of sustainability.

Procedural sustainability

The NRC (1999: 48) notes that sustainability is a 'process of social learning and adaptive response amidst turbulence and surprise.' This way of defining sustainability is referred to as *procedural sustainability* – a methodologically oriented approach that focuses on how sustainability comes to be defined and how pathways are developed to pursue it.

John Robinson, Associate Provost, Sustainability at the University of British Columbia, provides a succinct explanation of this view:

> The procedural [definition of sustainability] is that sustainability is the emergent property of a discussion about desired futures that's informed by some understanding of the ecological, social, and economic consequences of different courses of action.

Rather than being defined in thin, universalist terms, sustainability is defined through a participatory or democratic process contingent on place and time. As Norton (2005: 335) argues, '…the problem of how to measure sustainability… is logically subsequent to the prior question of what commitments the relevant community is willing to make to protect a natural and cultural legacy.'

Rotmans (former Director of DRIFT) also makes a case for procedural sustainability:

> [Sustainability] is very context-dependent… [I]n practical environments, my opinion is that what is sustainable is defined by the stakeholders that will be involved in this process… It means that it might be different in Rotterdam than in Amsterdam… [I]t's more the process itself where… you are continually making trade-offs in time, and in space, and in domains, and if you do that systematically and continuously, then the outcome for me doesn't matter as much as the process itself.

This is different from the participation of stakeholders in scientific research or the process of linking knowledge to action, which will be discussed below. Procedural sustainability is based on an understanding of sustainability as a process for identifying important societal values and pathways toward a desirable future. It emphasizes difference and context rather than agreement on a broad definition. It is not that procedural sustainability is in opposition to thin sustainability; rather, a thin definition is only useful insofar as it aids in the process of developing a contextual understanding of sustainability in a certain place or community.

Epistemic claims: research agendas for sustainability

Regardless of the way scientists define sustainability, there is widespread agreement (Lubchenco 1998; Palmer *et al.* 2004; Levin and Clark 2010) that science should contribute to sustainability efforts – 'promoting the goal of sustainability requires the emergence and conduct of the new field of sustainability science' (Friiberg 2000: 1). As both Matson and Clark noted in interviews, they adhere to a 'big tent' theory for what is to be included in sustainability, particularly at this point in its development. Two major themes in the construction of research agendas for sustainability are the *coupled systems approach* and the *social change approach*.

Coupled systems

Sustainability science 'seeks to understand the fundamental character of interactions between nature and society' (Kates *et al.* 2001: 641). As Carpenter *et al.* (2009: 1305) note, it is 'motivated by fundamental questions about interactions of nature and society as well as compelling and urgent social needs.' Likewise, Turner *et al.* (2003a: 8080) argue, '[s]ustainability science seeks understanding of the coupled human – environment system in ways that are useful to the different communities of stakeholders.' I refer to this set of research agendas as the *coupled systems* approach to sustainability science.

The coupled systems approach is focused on producing knowledge about 'the complex dynamics that arise from interactions between human and environmental systems' (Clark 2007: 1737). In its broadest sense, as B.L. Turner III of Arizona State University says, '[a]nything that fits under the rubric of how humankind is altering the basic structure and function of the earth's system… is a critical problem that ought to be studied.' The role of sustainability science, argues Parris of ISciences, is in 'understanding how [the human – environment system] functions.' Similarly, Elinor Ostrom, Nobel Laureate in Economics and a former editor of and contributor to the Sustainability Science section of *PNAS*, contends that sustainability science should be concerned with 'developing rigorous methods for analyzing complex systems over time.'

The coupled systems approach has several important implications for boundary work within science and its relationship to sustainability. It positions research on coupled human–natural systems as critical to efforts to move towards sustainability. For example, Clark (2010: 82) states that 'the *core* of sustainability science lies in seeking to understand how society's efforts to promote a transition toward sustainability are constrained or promoted by the interactions between human and environmental systems' (emphasis original). In order to adequately address the problems of sustainability, fundamental knowledge is required about the dynamics of coupled human–natural systems.[3] It is this knowledge that sustainability science can provide.

Clark (2010: 82) views sustainability science as problem-oriented yet grounded by a search for fundamental understanding of human–environment systems:

> Like 'agricultural science' and 'health science' before it, sustainability science is a field defined by the problems it addresses rather than the disciplines or methods it employs. For us, those problems are defined as the challenges of promoting a transition toward sustainability – improving human well-being while conserving the earth's life support systems over appropriate time and space scales. Sustainability science then draws from – and seeks to advance – those aspects of our understanding of human systems, environmental systems

and their interactions that are useful for helping people achieve sustainability goals.

This knowledge is produced in conjunction with stakeholders so that it is not just reliable but also salient, legitimate and trustworthy and thus more likely to assist society in making the transition to sustainability (Cash *et al.* 2006; Clark and Dickson 2003; Kates *et al.* 2001; NRC 1999). This leads to a final, key component of the coupled systems approach – connecting scientific research to practice, or linking knowledge to action (Cash *et al.* 2003).

However, as Matson noted in an interview, while 'a lot of progress has been made [in understanding life support systems]... there is going to be a lot more [research] needed in decision science, in behavioral research.' Knowledge of the system and its use in decision making is viewed as a factor limiting action. Part of the mission of sustainability science is to determine what knowledge is needed. This is done by basing on a better understanding of decision making and perceptions. How and why this knowledge is linked to societal action and what the implications are will be discussed in further detail below.

Social change

According to Jill Jäger, a researcher at the Sustainable Europe Research Institute, sustainability science 'is very much about process and very much about dialogue... it's a process for social change, learning, and transitions.' It should 'drive societal learning and change processes' and focus 'on the design and running of processes linking knowledge with action to deal with persistent problems of unsustainability and to foster transitions to sustainability' (Jäger 2009: 3). I refer to this as the *social change approach* to sustainability science.

The social change approach seeks to construct, inform and study processes for defining and pursuing sustainability. Rather than producing knowledge about underlying dynamics that are sustainable or unsustainable, it both produces knowledge about and actively participates in the processes of sustainability transitions. Paul Raskin, Director of the Tellus Institute, argues that we must focus on 'the ultimate drivers' that cause unsustainability or that might result in positive action – 'culture, power, politics and values.' Following the notion of procedural sustainability discussed earlier, Swart *et al.* (2004: 138) argue that sustainability science must 'emphasize the need to develop approaches for evaluating future options, recognizing diverse epistemologies and problem definitions, and encompassing the deeply normative nature of the sustainability problem.'

The social change approach is envisioned by some scientists as a mode of governance. The field of transitions management highlights this issue. Loorbach and Rotmans (2009: 240) define transitions management as 'a deliberative process to influence governance activities in such a way that they lead to accelerated change directed towards sustainability ambitions.' Derk Loorbach (2007: 18), current Director of DRIFT, defines a transition 'as a continuous process of societal change whereby the structure of society (or a subsystem of society) changes fundamentally.' Transitions management is a form of meta-governance – 'how do we influence, coordinate and bring together actors and their activities in such a way that they reinforce each other to such an extent that they can compete with dominant actors and practices?' (Loorbach and Rotmans 2009: 240).

This approach is concerned with how sectors of society or certain communities define sustainability in context, the process that facilitates a dialogue about this and the strategies that might be pursued to meet the goals that are set. While not always referred to as sustainability science by its adherents, it too is stakeholder-oriented, interdisciplinary and incorporates a systems perspective. The social change approach potentially creates a privileged role for science as a designer of and key participant in procedural sustainability. Epistemic authority emanates from knowledge shared and developed through the process of transitions management rather than knowledge about underlying system dynamics. It should, however, be noted that in focusing on the process it is recognized that there is a continual negotiation between actors about goals, knowledge and strategy for action. This approach creates a space for science as part of the process of sustainability and as a source of knowledge on how to design an effective process.

Socio-political claims: science and society

Regardless of the specific approach or research agenda, there is a consensus that science should respond to societal needs and the challenges of sustainability (Lubchenco 1998). Whether science is producing knowledge about complex coupled human–natural system dynamics or about processes for managing transition to sustainability, in each case science is a knowledge provider. But the role of knowledge in society, how it is developed and deployed, and how scientific knowledge is viewed relative to other types of knowledge, is complicated. If a primary goal of sustainability science is to help society make the transition to sustainability, it makes sense to ask: How might scientific knowledge help society solve problems and create solutions that will foster a transition to sustainability?

Building on the previous discussions, this section analyzes how scientists envision the knowledge produced by sustainability science contributing to society. Two broad themes emerged: the *knowledge-first* approach and the *process-oriented* approach.

Knowledge first

Cash *et al.* (2003: 8089) argue that, without drastically increasing the contribution of science and technology, 'it seems unlikely that the transition to sustainability will be either fast or far enough to prevent significant degradation of human life or the earth system.' Carpenter *et al.* (2009: 1305) contend that 'compelling and urgent social needs' stress 'the urgency and importance of accelerated effort to understand the dynamics of coupled human–natural systems.' Sustainability science performs fundamental research on problems identified by society which, scientists argue, will help move towards solutions. I refer to this vision of the role of science in society as the *knowledge-first approach*; i.e. 'science characterizes problems in terms of their causes and mechanisms as basis for subsequent action' (Sarewitz *et al.* 2010: 1).

As Matson (2009: 41) notes, 'the purposeful intent [of sustainability is] to link knowledge to action. Much of sustainability science is hard-core fundamental research, but the field is essentially use-inspired and oriented toward decision-making of all kinds.' Sustainability science, says Matson, can 'help make better decisions' but there has to be a 'pull' from decision makers. That is, decision makers have to signal to scientists what kind of information is needed to make better decisions. For example, Simon Levin of Princeton University and co-organizer of an NSF workshop on sustainable science, notes that scientists have 'no special expertise to deal with ethics, and certainly not with politics, so I see the role of scientists as not making decisions, but as informing decision makers.' Part of this process, then, is finding out what decision makers need.

This knowledge, it is argued, must be co-produced with stakeholders and decision makers. Co-production is *not* used here in the same sense as Jasanoff (2004) and others use the term in STS. In sustainability science co-production of knowledge refers to the act of producing information 'through the collaboration with scientists and engineers and nonscientists, who incorporate values and criteria from both communities' (Cash *et al.* 2006: 467). Organizing and facilitating co-production of knowledge at the interface of science and society is referred to as boundary management (Cash *et al.* 2003). These actions are meant to ensure the salience, credibility and legitimacy of the knowledge produced.

The knowledge-first approach views the problem of sustainability as a problem of not using available knowledge because it lacks credibility or legit-imacy, is insufficient or through not having knowledge about the necessary aspects of the system (salience). If science can provide the knowledge that is needed about coupled-system dynamics, for example, then better and more informed decisions may be made (i.e. decisions that will move society towards sustainability).

Sustainability scientists, however, are still careful to keep such activity separate from the core of the scientific research agenda – fundamental research into coupled human–natural systems. Being both 'basic' and 'applied,' knowledge-first sustainability science creates a boundary zone (see Figure 3.1) in which it justifies its usefulness to society and decision making for sustainability while maintaining epistemic authority by keeping its core research fundamental and free of values. As Kristjanson *et al.* (2009: 5049) conclude, 'there is certainly a role in sustainability science for both traditional, curiosity-driven research and for context-specific problem solving – so long as both are conducted within a larger framework that ensures rigor and usefulness.'

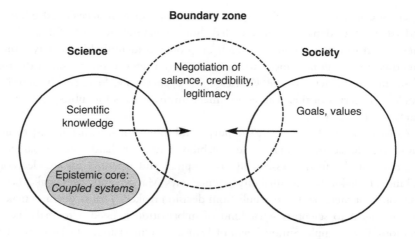

FIGURE 3.1 Knowledge-first sustainability, socio-political and epistemic claims (from Miller 2013).

The knowledge-first approach attempts both to be free of and to affect politics:

> Despite the awe in which we hold nature and the value we place on its conservation, ours is ultimately a project that seeks to understand what is, can be, and ought to be the human use of the earth. We pursue this goal, however, in the conviction that what is possible and desirable for people can only be understood through an appreciation of the interactions between social and environmental systems. (Clark 2010: 82; emphasis in original)

Through boundary work (in Gieryn's sense of the term) and boundary management, sustainability scientists attempt to externalize the potential risk politics pose to the epistemic core of sustainability science, while at the same time claiming to produce the knowledge that was heretofore limiting societal action.

Process-oriented approach

Lennart Olsson, Founding Director of the Lund University Centre for Sustainability Studies, argues that sustainability science can be called 'action research or... social intervention research... [in which scientists] intervene and then that intervention becomes [a subject] of study... [R]ather than... simply understanding... how do you actually feed into [the intervention]?' Here, the focus is on setting up, participating in and conducting research on social and technological processes that come to define and move towards sustainability goals. I refer to this approach as the *process-oriented* approach.

In some instances, the process-oriented approach goes beyond collaborative or participatory research to facilitating or actively participating in what Rotmans calls 'arenas for change or transition.' For example, in the field of transitions management, a 'transition arena' is created in which this work takes place. Loorbach and Rotmans (2009: 244) define a transition arena as an 'informal network... within which a group process unfolds, often in an unplanned and unforeseen way.' These arenas are sites for boundary management and the production of joint knowledge by scientists, decision makers and other stakeholders (Kemp and Rotmans 2009).

The aim of boundary management in this case is not necessarily to ensure that knowledge produced about coupled human–natural systems will be salient, credible and legitimate; rather, it is to facilitate a process for determining multiple trajectories for a transition and continual, mutual learning (Kemp and Rotmans 2009). There is an active role for science and scientists in establishing, facilitating and participating in mechanisms or dialogue for change, rather than simply providing knowledge from a more removed position.

Like the knowledge-first approach, in the process-oriented approach '[s]cience is still playing a big role in that first of all it's a knowledge provider,' says Jäger, 'but not the only knowledge provider.' Robinson makes a similar point: 'Science plays the crucial role of providing some of the information about consequences and trade-offs associated with difference choices, but it doesn't tell us anything about where we want to be. That has to emerge from discussion... We [scientists] want to engage them as citizens of part of a collective.' The role of science is to help society or communities deliberate over what sustainability might look like and how communities might move towards it. Both the knowledge-first and the process-oriented approaches are concerned with assisting a sustainability transition by producing credible knowledge. Most sustainability scientists acknowledge the importance of working with stakeholders so that science can provide useful information. However, how they envision the type of knowledge needed and the role of that knowledge in assisting society are quite different.

David Kriebel, co-Director of the Lowell Center for Sustainable Production, cautions that '[scientists] have to be aware not to allow the need to fully characterize the system delay action.' He believes that it is important to make a 'distinction between the system in which the problem occurs and the system in which the solution occurs.' By focusing on where the solution may occur, he argues, the conversation shifts from a scientific characterization of the system to the social, political, economic and technological processes involved in formulating a desirable outcome. In Jäger's words, 'it's trying to find ways to get things done.'

In response to a question on the role of sustainability science in society, Robinson asks, '[w]ho needs to know the science?' He sketches three potential ways in which scientists might seek to help society move towards sustainability. The first potential method would be to use guilt to pressure individuals into changing their behavior, which, he notes, has not been terribly successful thus far. A second would be 'to do a brilliant analysis, and it's so compelling and convincing that when we give it to policy makers, they change everything.' In his own experience, however, Robinson argues that the role of science 'has to be [in] a conversation where various forms of certified knowledge are brought together with various ethical and normative views of citizens… in an exploration of where we want to be in the future.'

The process-oriented approach at once creates a space for science as a source of credible knowledge and limits its own epistemic authority by acknowledging that it is just one source of such knowledge among many. Scientific analysis is broadly focused on the process of envisioning and pursuing pathways to sustainability (e.g. Robinson and Tansey 2006). Rather than knowledge acting as the factor limiting the ability to make decisions, it is a matter of constructing a social process in which various forms of credible knowledge, perspectives and values can come together to define sustainability. This creates a more open discourse about what sustainability is and how a given community might move towards it (see Figure 3.2). The process-oriented approach is more concerned with exploring pathways to sustainability than with maintaining a core program of fundamental research.

Bounding sustainability

In both the universalist and the procedural definitions of sustainability, scientists are carving out a role for science and shaping the way society might understand sustainability. For thin sustainability, a universal understanding of sustainability is complemented by the universal applicability of science – 'the only universal discourse available in a multiply fragmented world' (Jasanoff 1996: 173). There is a normative distancing of a value-free epistemic core from the value-laden questions of sustainability. This limits not just the debate over the appropriate or effective role of science but also important social, political and cultural debates over the nature of sustainability, especially in specific contexts. Sustainability is prevented from becoming 'thick' because science cannot go there; science cannot become contextual, contested and qualified.

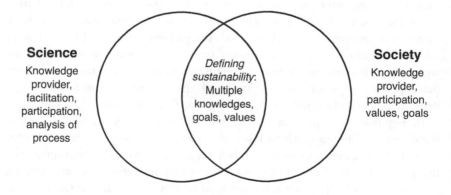

FIGURE 3.2 Process-oriented sustainability science (from Miller 2013).

TABLE 3.1 Boundary work and claims in sustainability science.

	Universalist	*Procedural*
Normative claims	• Normative frame • Universal values • "Value-free" science	• Defining as process • Values of community • Contextual
	Coupled Systems	*Social Change*
Epistemic claims	• Fundamental research • Social needs • Co-production of knowledge with stakeholders	• Action research • Processes of transitions • Participant
	Knowledge-first	*Process-oriented*
Socio-political	• Problem space • Salient, credible, legitimate knowledge • Knowledge provider	• Social intervention • Beyond understanding • Facilitate and participate in process

As Jamieson (1998: 189) argues, at this universal level 'there is too little by way of shared beliefs and values to provide enough content to ideas of sustainability to make them effective.' Procedural sustainability, on the other hand, attempts to identify social values that are important for sustainability that will result in action. According to Norton (2005: 405) the question that a more procedural sustainability can help address is 'how can diverse, democratic communities develop procedures that encourage cooperative action to protect their environment?' Considered in the light of procedural sustainability, the process–oriented approach to the relationship between science and society establishes a dual role for science as both participant and observer of the procedures Norton proposes.

In order to address the problems of sustainability, Cash *et al.* (2003) urge that society 'harness the power of science and technology.' Both the coupled systems and social change approaches to sustainability make 'compelling arguments for why science is uniquely best as a provider of trustworthy knowledge, and compelling narratives for why [their] science is bona fide' (Gieryn 1999: 4). The coupled systems approach does this by maintaining a core of basic science while conceding that it must also be applied in order to link knowledge to action. The social change approach is more critical of the usefulness of science, yet it carefully maintains a space as part of societal processes that define sustainability *and* as uniquely positioned to analyze such processes.

Scientists, particularly in the coupled systems approach, seek to establish their epistemic authority over facts about the sustainability of system dynamics and the approach's usefulness in decision making. At the same time, they both site a thin sustainability as a normative goal or motivation *and* establish normative discussions as outside of the realm of hard-core science. Boundary work performed by sustainability scientists delineates the analysis of coupled human–natural systems as the scientific purview of sustainability science. The coupled systems approach is similar to what Thompson (2010) refers to as functional integrity. Functional integrity can be 'understood in terms of threats to or failures in the integrity of functional systems on which they depend' (Thompson 2010: 221). This leads to a perspective that certain human activities are sustainable or unsustainable as determined by the ways in which they affect this functional integrity. As Jasanoff and Wynne (1998: 25) note, '[t]he universalism of technical discourses is often maintained through scientists' unstated naturalization of their own assumptions concerning social behavior; that is, scientists come to accept their own assumptions as natural and not open to question.'

Given the complexity of these systems, science is relied upon to reveal and translate for society. This leads to the second act of boundary work – sustainability scientists imagine the effective pursuit of sustainability as requiring fundamental knowledge about coupled systems that sustainability science provides. However, as environmental philosopher Mark Sagoff (2008) warns, there is a danger in relying too heavily on science in areas that he argues are primarily of ethical concern. For example, Sagoff (2008: 207) argues that environmental science 'presents nature as a system for interdisciplinary scientists to model and administer for the collective good rather than as an object for moral instruction and aesthetic appreciation for every individual.'

Exploring how scientists are constructing research agendas for sustainability, this chapter presents an opportunity to take stock of recent, rapid developments and pose the question 'how is sustainability science to be positioned to assist society in a sustainability transition?' While certainly not discounting the substantial and thoughtful efforts that have gone into the development of the field, this analysis offers an opportunity to continue a dialogue about sustainability science in new directions. Where, for example, is scientific knowledge a limiting factor in decision making? Where will fundamental understanding of human–natural systems enhance our capacity to make decisions? What other factors are limiting decision making and how will science affect that context? How is science to be engaged in the social, political and ethical components of sustainability while maintaining its ability to provide credible knowledge where needed? What can the approaches outlined here offer each other?

This chapter has shown how different visions of sustainability science are emerging with different values, knowledge and socio-political claims (Table 3.1). These claims have implications for the credibility of different styles of sustainability science under alternative normative positions, including how the field is positioned with regards to more radical notions of social change. The following chapter explores the implications of current trajectories in sustainability science, laying the foundation for the reconstruction of sustainability science.

Notes

1 Parts of this chapter have been published previously (Miller, Thaddeus R. 2013. Constructing sustainability science: Emerging perspectives and research trajectories. *Sustainability Science* 8(2): 279–93) and have been published here with permission.
2 Walzer borrows this term from Geertz's (1973) 'thick description.' Walzer's (1994: xi) aim, however, is not to present a thick description of moral argument but to refer to argument that is thick – 'richly referential, culturally resonant, locked into locally established symbolic systems or network of meanings.'
3 Coupled human–natural systems are also referred to as human–environment or social-ecological systems. They are broadly defined as 'integrated systems in which people interact with natural components' (Liu *et al.* 2007: 1513).

References

Beck, U. 1992. *The risk society: Towards a new modernity.* London: Sage.
Carpenter, S.R., A. Harold, J.A. Mooney, D. Capistrano, R.S. DeFries, S. Diaz, T. Dietz, K. Anantha, A.O. Duraiappah, H.M. Pereira, C. Perrings, W.V. Reid, J. Sarukhan, R.J. Scholes, and A. Whyte. 2009. Science for managing ecosystem services: beyond the Millennium Ecosystem Assessment. *Proceedings of the National Academy of Sciences* 106(5): 1305–12.
Cash, D.W., W.C. Clark, F. Alcock, N.M. Dickson, N. Eckley, D.H. Guston, J. Jäger, and R.B. Mitchell. 2003. Knowledge systems for sustainable development. *Proceedings of the National Academy of Sciences of the United States of America* 100(14) (July 8): 8086–91.
Cash, D.W., J.C. Borck, and A.G. Patt. 2006. Countering the loading-dock approach to linking science and decision making: Comparative analysis of El Niño/Southern Oscillation (ENSO) forecasting systems. *Science, Technology and Human Values* 31(4): 465–94.
Clark, W.C. 2007. Sustainability science: A room of its own. *Proceedings of the National Academy of Sciences* 104(6): 1737–8.
Clark, W.C. 2010. Sustainable development and sustainability science. In report from Toward a Science of Sustainability Conference, Airlie Center, Warrenton, VA (2009).
Clark, W.C. and N.M. Dickson. 2003. Sustainability science: The emerging research program. *Proceedings of the National Academy of Sciences of the United States of America* 100(14) (July 8): 8059–61.
Collingridge, D. and C. Reeve. 1986. *Science speaks to power: The role of experts in policy.* New York: St Martin's Press.
Friiberg Workshop Report. 2000. Sustainability science. Statement of the Friiberg Workshop on Sustainability Science, Friiberg, Sweden.
Geertz, C. 1973. *The interpretation of cultures.* New York: Basic Books.
Gieryn, T. 1999. *Cultural boundaries of science: Credibility on the line.* Chicago, London: University of Chicago Press.
Hassan, M. 2001. Transition to sustainability in the twenty-first century: the contribution of science and technology – Report of the World Conference of Scientific Academies held in Tokyo, Japan, 15–18 May 2000. *International Journal of Sustainability in Higher Education* 2(1): 70–78.
Jäger, J. 2009. Sustainability science in Europe. (Background paper prepared for European Commission's DG for Research). Available at: http://seri.at/wp-content/uploads/2009/11/Sustainability-Science-in-Europe.pdf.
Jamieson, D. 1995. Ecosystem health: Some preventive medicine. *Environmental Values* 4(4): 333–44.

Jamieson, D. 1998. Sustainability and beyond. *Ecological Economics* 24: 183–92.

Jasanoff, S. 1987. Contested boundaries in policy-relevant science. *Social Studies of Science* 17(2): 195–230.

Jasanoff, S. 1996. Science and norms in global environmental regimes. In Fen Osler Hampson and Judith Reppy, (eds), *Earthly Goods: Environmental Change and Social Justice*, pp 173–97. Ithaca, NY: Cornell University Press.

Jasanaoff, S. 2004. Ordering knowledge, ordering society. In Sheila Jasanoff, (ed.), *States of knowledge: The co-production of science and social order*, pp 274–82. New York: Routledge.

Jasanoff, S. and B. Wynne. 1998. Science and decisionmaking. In Steve Rayner and Elizabeth Malone, (eds), *Human Choice and Climate Change, Vol. 1: The Societal Framework*, pp 1–87. Columbus, OH: Battelle Press.

Kates, R.W., W.C. Clark, R. Corell, J.M. Hall, C.C. Jaeger, I. Lowe, J.J. McCarthy, H.J. Schellnhuber, B. Bolin, N.M. Dickson, S. Faucheux, G.C. Gallopin, A. Grübler, B. Huntley, J. Jäger, N.S. Jodha, R.E. Kasperson, A. Mabogunje, P. Matson, H. Mooney, B. Moore III, T. O'Riordan, and U. Svedin. 2001. Sustainability science. *Science* 292(5517): 641–2.

Kemp, R. and J. Rotmans. 2009. Transitioning policy: Co-production of a new strategic framework for energy innovation policy in the Netherlands. *Policy Science* 42: 303–22.

Kristjanson, P., R.S. Reid, N. Dickson, W.C. Clark, D. Romney, R. Puskur, S. MacMillan, and D. Grace. 2009. Linking international agricultural research knowledge with action for sustainable development. *Proceedings of the National Academy of Sciences of the United States of America* 106(13): 5047–52.

Levin, S.A. and W.C. Clark 2010. *Toward a science of sustainability*. Report from Toward a Science of Sustainability Conference, Airlie Center, Warrenton, VA, (2009).

Liu, J., T. Dietz, S.R. Carpenter, M. Alberti, C. Folke, E. Moran, A.N. Pell, P. Deadman, T. Kratz, J. Lubchenco, E. Ostrom, Z. Ouyang, W. Provencher, C.L. Redman, S. Schneider, W.W. Taylor. 2007. Complexity of coupled human and natural systems. *Science* 317: 1513.

Loorbach, D. 2007. *Transitions management: New mode of governance for sustainable development*. Utrecht, Netherlands: International Books.

Loorbach, D. and J. Rotmans. 2009. The practice of transitions management: Examples and lessons from four distinct cases. *Futures* 42(3): 237–46.

Lubchenco, J. 1998. Entering the century of the environment: A new social contract for science. *Science* 279(5350): 491.

Matson, P. 2009. The sustainability transition. *Issues in Science and Technology* Summer 2009: 39–42.

Miller, T.R. 2013. Constructing sustainability science: Emerging perspectives and research trajectories. *Sustainability Science* 8(2): 279–93.

National Research Council. 1999. *Our common journey: A transition toward sustainability*. Washington, DC: National Academy Press.

Norton, B.G. 2005. *Sustainability: A philosophy of adaptive ecosystem management*. Chicago: University of Chicago Press.

Ostrom, E. 2007. A diagnostic approach for going beyond panaceas. *Proceedings of the National Academy of Sciences of the United States of America* 104(39): 15181–7.

Palmer, M., E. Bernhardt, E. Chornesky, S. Collins, A. Dobson, C. Duke, B. Gold, R. Jacobson, S. Kingsland, R. Kranz, M. Mappin, M.L. Martinez, F. Micheli, J. Morse, M. Pace, M. Pascual, S. Palumbi, O.J. Reichman, A. Simons, A. Townsend, M. Turner. 2004. Ecology for a crowded planet. *Science* 304(5675): 1251–2.

Parris, T.M. and R.W. Kates. 2003. Characterizing a sustainability transition: Goals, targets, trends, and driving forces. *Proceedings of the National Academy of Sciences* 100: 8068.

Robinson, J. and J. Tansey. 2006. Co-production, emergent properties and strong interactive social research: The Georgia Basic Futures Project. *Science and Public Policy* 33(2): 151–60.

Sagoff, M. 2008. *The economy of the earth: Philosophy, law, and the environment*, 2nd edn. Cambridge: Cambridge University Press.

Sarewitz, D., D. Kriebel, R. Clapp, C. Crumbley, P. Hoppin, M. Jacobs, and J. Tickner. 2010. The sustainable solutions agenda. Consortium for Science, Policy and Outcomes and Lowell Center for Sustainable Production, Arizona State University and University of Massachusetts, Lowell.

Swart, R., P. Raskin, and J. Robinson. 2004. Critical challenges for sustainability science. *Science* 297(5589): 1994–5.

Thompson, P.B. 2010. *The agrarian vision: Sustainability and environmental ethics*. Lexington, KY: University of Kentucky Press.

Turner, B.L. II, P.A. Matson, J.J. McCarthy, R.W. Corell, L. Christensen, N. Eckley, G.K. Hovelsrud-Broda, J.X. Kasperson, R.E. Kasperson, A. Luers, M.L. Martello, S. Mathiesen, R. Naylor, C. Polsky, A. Pulsipher, A. Schiller, H. Selin, and N. Tyler. 2003a. Illustrating the coupled human–environment system for vulnerability analysis: Three case studies. *Proceedings of the National Academy of Sciences* 100(14): 8080–85.

Walzer, M. 1994. *Thick and thin: Moral argument at home and abroad*. South Bend, IN: University of Notre Dame Press.

4

TENSIONS IN SUSTAINABILITY SCIENCE

The crux of the sustainability challenge facing humanity in the twenty-first century is the ability to reconcile continued improvement in human welfare around the globe with the capacity of natural systems to support such development. It is this grand challenge that the allied concepts of sustainable development and sustainability attempt to articulate. This challenge has gained significant traction in the scientific community over the last decade as scientists have attempted to formulate research agendas in response to what they view as the problems of sustainability (e.g. Holling 2001; Lubchenco 1998; Mihelcic et al. 2003; NRC 1999; Palmer et al. 2005; Schellnhuber et al. 2004).

Many scientists have argued that the problems of sustainability, from climate change and biodiversity loss to poverty alleviation and access to adequate safe water supplies, require renewed effort on the part of the scientific community to conduct research on the issues that matter most to society. Scientists stress the urgency of harnessing the contributions of science and technology as a means for developing solutions to sustainability problems (e.g. Cash et al. 2003; Clark et al. 2002; Kates et al. 2001; Hardin 1993; Leshner 2002; Reid et al. 2010).

To this point, Part I has examined these developments – to take stock of emerging visions for the field, and to create a reflexive distance from which to explore tensions, limitations and alternative pathways for sustainability science. The research goals of sustainability science – fundamental research on complex human–natural systems – and its stated mission – linking knowledge to action for sustainability – are often assumed to be synergistic by sustainability scientists. Following the results presented in Chapter 3, this chapter explores underlying tensions that, if navigated poorly, will devalue important normative debates about sustainability goals, elevating some norms (for instance, narrower technical and scientific values) over broader societal norms (responsibility to nature and future generations, for example), and inhibit the ability of sustainability scientists to perform research that will foster beneficial societal outcomes.

Tensions in sustainability science

The ways in which sustainability scientists contest or lay claim to normative, epistemic or socio-political arguments shape not only the research agenda for the field but also its ability to deal with contested values that inevitably arise around sustainability issues and to link knowledge to action. The first such tension that emerges from this analysis of boundary work is between science and the normative nature of sustainability – the potential consequences of transforming sustainability, a normative, contested and ambiguous concept, into the subject of scientific analysis. Sustainability can provide communities with a conceptual framework within which to articulate and pursue visions of social and natural well-being (Norton 2005). The role of science in fostering such efforts is not straightforward, however. Science can provide descriptive foundations for normative statements in favor of sustaining ecosystem resilience or adaptive capacity, for example; but, science, through the perceived epistemic authority of its explanations, can also limit what is considered appropriate discourse (Appadurai 1996; Smith 2009). For instance, scientific explanations of climate change and atmospheric dynamics, and not more local or regional explanations and approaches such as adaption (Pielke, Jr *et al.* 2007), have served to underpin a global understanding of climate and the mitigation of greenhouse gases as a potential solution. Science can both *enable* and *constrain* discourse about problems and their potential solutions.

This is a tension between the scientific and technical complexity of coupled systems and the social or community values that define sustainability for a given community. Often, the problem is not related to a need for more knowledge, as Matson hinted in an earlier quotation. Instead, it may be that myriad other social, political, technological or ethical issues require resolution. This is not to say that scientific knowledge will not help to make decisions better informed or even lead to convergence on a decision in certain situations. At the extreme, sustainability science may 'black box' sustainability as a scientific and technical issue (Latour 1987; Winner 1986).

The second tension revolves around the issue of what is known about the institutional and epistemological contexts that link knowledge to societal outcomes. The popularly assumed relationship in the linear model discussed around Figure 2.2 is that more knowledge will lead to better decisions. The role of scientific knowledge in decision making is much more complicated, however (Collingridge and Reeve 1986; Jasanoff 1990). There may be numerous factors at play in affecting decision-making capacity in any given context, the least of which is the level or certainty of scientific knowledge. This is the tension between *knowledge* and *action*.

Thomas Kuhn (1977, later edition 1996) uses the notion of essential tensions to great effect to illustrate the conservative and innovative imperatives of science. Scientists, argues Kuhn, must be able to solve puzzles effectively within a given paradigm. The practice of normal science 'is a highly convergent activity based firmly upon a settled consensus acquired from scientific education and reinforced by subsequent life in the profession' (Kuhn 1977: 227). Nonetheless, divergent thinking is necessary when scientists must grapple with and seek to explain anomalies that do not fit their traditional paradigm.

In Kuhn's view, the tension between the necessity of convergent thinking for the practice of everyday science and divergent thinking for innovation in the pursuit of anomalies is essential to the advancement of scientific knowledge. Crucial to Kuhn's thinking on this point is that innovation and paradigm shifts will not occur without the convergent standards of normal science to support the ability of scientists to recognize novelty. Occasionally, as a crisis occurs when the current paradigm cannot explain anomalies, 'scientists must be able to live in a world out of joint' (Kuhn 1996: 79).

Social studies of science scholars have also used the idea of tensions to illustrate various aspects of scientific research in practice. Hackett (2005), for example, explores the systemic tensions that research groups must navigate, including those between autonomy and control in managing a research lab, and between novelty, accepted methods and problems in the pursuit of research pathways. The concerns of Kuhn and Hackett have focused primarily on the internal dynamics of science – the array of social and institutional forces that pull at scientists as they perform research. Here, the focus is not on the social forces internal to science; it is on the tensions that emerge as scientists attempt to perform research on issues of societal importance and link scientific knowledge to social outcomes.

There is a pervasive belief – particularly among scientists – that more scientific knowledge is necessary to achieve beneficial outcomes (Collingridge and Reeve 1986; Neff 2011; Nelson 2003). This chapter explores the tensions between the knowledge produced by sustainability science and the use of that knowledge by society. By bringing these tensions to light, they may be more effectively navigated by sustainability scientists and contribute to the reconstruction of a more effective and reflexive agenda for sustainability.

The enabling and constraining power of science

'The substantive focus of sustainability science,' states Matson (2009: 39), 'is on the complex dynamics of the coupled human/environment system.' It is also, as Clark (2010: 82) states, 'ultimately a project that seeks to understand what is, can be, and ought to be the human use of the earth.' This is a starkly social, ethical and political choice about what to sustain, for whom and for how long. However, normative distancing by scientists can obscure the degree to which socio-political issues are masked by science, or overstate how far scientific knowledge can help make such hard choices. It is important to consider how the fundamental research goals of sustainability science and its commitment to contributing to more sustainable outcomes might affect the understanding and pursuit of sustainability values and goals. Sustainability scientists, concerned STS scholars, and decision makers and publics must be aware of how the epistemic and normative commitments of sustainability scientists shape societal understandings of sustainability (and vice versa). At the core of this issue lies a tension between the capability of science to both reveal what were previously unobservable phenomena and constrain the variety of alternative legitimate explanations for those phenomena. As STS have shown, the ways in which we come to know the world also shape it, including how we value it (Jasanoff 2004b; Latour 1993; Shapin and Schaffer 1985). The following discussion explores the implications of subjecting a contingent, contextual, contested and value-laden concept – sustainability – to objective, empirical scientific analysis.

Communities focused on environmental and sustainability issues have traditionally relied on science to reveal problems and defend solutions (Bocking 2004; Jasanoff 2004b). Science can help to illuminate new realms of ethical concern. Concerns for sustainability and intergenerational equity, for instance, were driven in part by inquiries into climate change and other long-term environmental impacts (Sarewitz 1996). The role of scientific knowledge and expertise in such issues, however, is much more complex (Callon *et al.* 2011). Science can reveal more uncertainty and support multiple value positions that may in fact exacerbate the difficulty of resolving problems (Jasanoff 1990; Sarewitz 2004).

Additionally, there is often a gap between how scientists think about a problem and how the public comes to know or understand it – what Jasanoff (2005) and Miller (2008) refer to as civic epistemologies. Civic epistemologies are 'the social and institutional practices by which political communities construct, review, validate, and deliberate politically relevant knowledge' (Miller 2008: 1896). The process by which political communities make knowledge and how it is argued, reasoned, promoted and utilized in public deliberation over sustainability goals and indicators (Miller 2005) are different from the social and institutional arrangements and epistemic commitments of the scientific community.

Further, as Dupré (1993) notes, 'science aims to detect order and to create order.' The way in which science interrogates an issue can impact the way that issue is framed by policy and the public (Bocking 2004; Miller 2008). The ways scientists frame problems may not make for the most effective or democratic social outcome. The goals – to advance knowledge, disciplinary expertise – and institutional context – to publish in an area of expertise, to gain tenure – of science and scientists may actually serve as constraints on acting pragmatically, which can be defined in terms of social action by way of policy or politics that might advance visions of sustainability. As sustainability science continues to develop as a field, it makes choices about what aspects of coupled systems to examine and how. As it does this, sustainability scientists may exclude other ways of knowing, often unwittingly.

At one level, this is the classic tension between the technical nature of environmental (and sustainability) problems and the need and desire for transparency and democratic deliberation (Bocking 2004; Brown 2009; Fischer 2000). My concern is slightly subtler, engaging the epistemic nature of this tension. Sustainability science, like all empirical work, requires the development of ways to categorize the world (Bowker and Star 1999; Cartwright 1999; Porter 1995; Scott 1998). Scientific communities do not just seek knowledge about nature, they seek knowledge about nature under a specific description – e.g. teleological, mechanistic or as a complex adaptive system (Longino 1990). Before any knowledge is produced or any research performed, the system under inquiry must be characterized 'in ways that make certain kinds of explanation appropriate and others inappropriate' (Longino 1990: 98).

In its quest for understanding, science disciplines problems, making them amenable to certain methodological approaches and theoretical frameworks. Nonetheless, often the difficulty of finding solutions for many sustainability problems is not related to an inadequacy of scientific knowledge. A better understanding of a given issue may not succeed in taming a wicked problem or in making it any more amenable to social, political and technological solutions. Sustainability science has, however, made a promising move towards place-based research that attempts to address concerns as scales that are socially significant.

How sustainability science disciplines the issues with which it is concerned will make those issues more or less tractable, more open or closed to debate. This is a problem for sustainability science if it intends to contribute to societal efforts to pursue sustainability transitions because other scientific ways of understanding and value-based perspectives are excluded. Robbins (2001), for example, tells the story of a satellite image of a small town in India. Robbins showed this image to several of the town's inhabitants, evoking myriad interpretations. Foresters pointed to evidence of reforestation; farmers noted the bare soils and denuded areas; a retired forester lamented the loss of tree cover; and a worker at a local advocacy organization for pastoralists cited the amount of grassland that had been lost to increased tree cover.

This single satellite image highlights the plurality of interpretations of categories in the landscape. Seemingly simple concepts that many scientists take for granted such as 'forest,' 'degraded' and 'grassland' are contested. Satellite imagery is not an impartial, objective tool. Rather, imagery itself is both a political tool used to settle categories in the landscape and a force for transforming the environment. In Robbins's account, the result is the extension of green canopy cover with little human or ecosystem value. The scientists' categories become normalized and objective as they are repeated (Anderson 1991; Porter 1995). As Robbins argues, '[t]he measurement of these resulting landscapes through the very tools of their transformation [i.e. satellite imagery] naturalizes the resulting ecologies and erases the history of intervention from which they arise' (Robbins 2001: 176). The erasure of this history transforms contested categories of change in land use and land cover into black boxes (Latour 1987). They become accepted facts in landscape management rather than contested categories that are open to interpretation and that embody different practices and livelihoods.

Science has the power to constrain discussions of contested concepts and categories. It influences what counts as 'real' in the world. Scientists, perhaps necessarily, take reductionist approaches as they search for causal mechanisms, analyze problems and advance knowledge. This constraining power of science has implications for the ability of communities to voice legitimate normative perspectives about their future and how we understand phenomena that may impact those perspectives (i.e. what is sustainable or not in a given context), especially when it comes to wicked problems.

The categories scientists create are adopted by social actors in unpredictable and unintended ways (Porter 1995). James Scott (1998) details the rise of scientific forestry in late-eighteenth-century Germany. State-managed forest science transformed a dynamic and diverse old-growth forest into a uniform, legible, mono-cropped grid of board feet of timber, an ecosystem and cultural domain into a volume of lumber. As Scott (1998: 15) notes, 'the German forest became the archetype for imposing on disorderly nature the neatly arranged constructs of science.' Germany forestry science came to dominate the curriculum of American and European forestry schools, shaping both science and forest management on both continents for the next century.

While successful in the short run, this utopian vision of a regimented forest producing a sustained yield of lumber under the tutelage of scientific forestry eventually met with the more complex reality of the diverse ecological processes required to support a healthy forest. In the worst cases, the result was *Waldsterben*, forest death. Scott's account (1998: 21) 'illustrates the dangers of dismembering an exceptionally complex and poorly understood set of relations and processes in order to isolate a single element of instrumental value.' As Thompson (2010: 239) notes, many scientists argue that:

> advanced systems modeling is a wholly value-free process that will, through pure science, generate the information we need to save the planet... but... the way we conceptualize a system is deeply value laden and reflects judgments about what is thought to be problematic, as well as likely guesses about where the solutions might lie.

Forest scientists simplified German forests to maximize yields; so, too must sustainability science produce simplifications to make wicked problems amenable to empirical analysis.

Positioning the understanding of complex, coupled human–natural systems as crucial to efforts to move toward sustainability, sustainability scientists also put themselves in an epistemically superior position. Sustainability scientists presumably hold the key to helping society move toward sustainability. Through their theories and methods, society is able to gain access into the workings of complex systems. The pursuit of the community-defined goals for sustainability, however, is not equivalent to the realization of scientifically objective goods. The danger lies not just with the simplifications that may be necessary to make the dynamics of complex, coupled human–natural systems the object of scientific analysis, but also in effects of sustainability science on value debates in society. Societal efforts to articulate and pursue sustainability require a certain discursive and conceptual 'breathing room' that allows for an open deliberation of aims and value commitments.

Sagoff (2008), for instance, highlights the issues that arise between science and value-laden pursuits such as sustainability. He argues that environmentalists have relied too heavily on scientific theories and facts in what are essentially value-based arguments about aesthetics and environmental health. Environmentalism now,

> appeals to theories of the structure and function of ecosystems, the balance of nature, and other scientific principles... to prescribe values to society rather than to respond to values society already had... Environmentalism insofar as it relies on scientific theories or postulates has little to do with the places – particular forests or vistas – that people know, care about, or what to protect (Sagoff 2008: 205).

Similarly, Jamieson (1995) and others (Schrader-Frechette and McCoy 1994; Worster 1993) critique attempts to base environmental goals on science. For example, Jamieson (1995) argues that the concept of ecosystem health works to objectify our preferences related to ecosystem values. Such efforts are themselves unlikely to succeed in providing an objective basis for ecosystem management because our preferences and values related to ecosystems, like those related to human health, are contextual and unstable. Efforts to found on science value-based goals, whether they be environmental, sustainability or otherwise, are not only ontologically and epistemologically dubious – defining ecosystem health or sustainability scientifically is often, if not always, extremely difficult or impossible – they are also normatively and politically undesirable, limiting the ability to legitimately express conflicts about what is valued.

Scientists purport to focus on the facts – i.e. the dynamics of coupled systems – while society and decision makers deal with the realm of values – i.e. what is to be sustained. Sustainability scientists attempt to address value-laden, wicked problems while maintaining a pristine, epistemic core of fundamental research. For example, for Clark (2010: 82) 'the *core* of sustainability science lies in seeking to understand how society's efforts to promote a transition toward sustainability are constrained or promoted by the interactions between human and environmental systems' (emphasis in original). By placing the understanding of coupled human–natural systems at the center of the research agenda, sustainability science is given access to understanding complex system dynamics. This framing has the effect of privileging sustainability science over alternative understandings of such dynamics in larger sustainability debates. It becomes less important to have discussions over potential future pathways for a community; instead, sustainability science can *know* what dynamics are (un)sustainable and deliver that information to society. Value debates are rendered impotent through the threat of incontestable nature (Latour 2004).

Scientists, policy makers and the public are rarely aware of how the ways in which science categorizes the world also work to shape it (Jasanoff 2005). As Longino (2002: 189) notes, '[a]fter consensus, the constructive role of scientists disappears, and the result or theory is seen as inevitable, an expression of nature.' It becomes black-boxed (Latour 1987). While necessary for the advancement of scientific knowledge, this eliminates the plurality of values within the sustainability discourse and constrains the number of legitimate voices and explanations for the sources of and solutions to various problems. Conceptualizing social problems in scientific and technological terms can confuse or eliminate cultural, political and normative discussions through the value-neutral, objective language of science (Fischer 2000; Jamieson 1995). Elucidating these tensions is a step toward enhancing the reflexivity of sustainability science and societal efforts to achieve sustainability goals.

Avoiding the knowledge-first trap

A key characteristic of sustainability science is the effort to link scientific knowledge with societal action (Cash *et al.* 2003; Clark 2007; Kates *et al.* 2001; Matson 2009). Sustainability scientists are driven not just by fundamental research questions but also by performing research on pressing social and environmental problems (Clark and Dickson 2003; Levin and Clark 2010). As Carpenter *et al.* (2009: 1305) state, 'sustainability science is motivated by fundamental questions about interactions of nature and society as well as compelling and urgent social needs.' They continue, arguing that the challenges of sustainability highlight 'the urgency and importance of accelerated effort to understand the dynamics of coupled human–natural systems.' Similarly, Matson (2009: 41) views the 'purposeful intent to link knowledge to action' as a core component of sustainability science. While 'much of sustainability is hard-core fundamental research,' notes Matson (2009: 41), 'it is essentially use-inspired and is oriented towards decisionmaking of all sorts.' Sustainability scientists assume that science will support the pursuit of sustainability values and that knowledge about coupled human–natural systems will lead to better, more sustainable decisions. This dynamic is not unique to sustainability science, of course.

Underlying these efforts are two interrelated assumptions about the relationship between scientific knowledge and decision making for sustainability:

1 scientific knowledge is necessary and may even compel action relative to sustainability goals; and
2 sustainability science and its focus on fundamental questions in coupled human–natural systems dynamics can provide that knowledge.

The first has to do with the diagnosis of the factors limiting the ability of society to take action relative to sustainability goals – i.e. a lack of scientific knowledge. As Cash *et al.* (2003: 8086) argue, '[a] capacity for mobilizing and using science and technology is increasingly recognized as an essential component of strategies for promoting sustainable development.' Similarly, in a study of research priorities in ecology, Neff (2011: 467) finds that many ecologists believe that 'amassing a preponderance of evidence about anthropogenic impacts… can compel leaders to make "better" policies and decisions.' Additional knowledge is required to make decisions that will be more sustainable. The second assumption is that science, and in this case, sustainability science, can provide the knowledge about coupled system dynamics needed to contribute to decision making and improve decisions. Miller and Neff (2013) review these results in a discussion of how the normative and epistemic concerns of scientists guide science policy in-the-making.

A brief examination of what Nelson (1977) refers to as the 'science and technology policy perspective' will serve to further illuminate these assumptions and the potential tension between knowledge and decision making. The key intellectual commitment of this perspective is that many problems can be solved with the proper application of scientific knowledge and technological capabilities. It is only a matter of directing research towards the appropriate goals. However, as Nelson (1977: 62) notes,

> [w]hile formally trained scientists and engineers, engaged in organized research and development, have been remarkably effective in advancing knowledge and creating powerful new capabilities in certain selected arenas, there is a strong element of faith attached to the proposition that these kinds of talents and activities can be applied powerfully to the solution of most any problem.

Nelson uses the example of crime and education. While the ability to address each of these problems may be limited by knowledge in some way, it is doubtful that the application of natural science or engineering could wholly address such issues. As Nelson (2003) notes, this is not a comment on researchers in the field of education (or in sustainability science for that matter). Instead, it has to do with limitations of the ability of research to contribute to areas where progress is largely tacit (i.e. relies on experience and practice) and social.

In this simplified model of the relationship between science and action, scientific knowledge provides the understanding on which decisions can be made (Komiyama and Takeuchi 2006; Levin and Clark 2010; Sumi 2007; Palmer *et al.* 2004; Parris and Kates 2003). Mooney and Sala (1993: 566), for instance, contend that better science will lead to more sustainable use of natural resources – '[w]e conclude that sustainable use of resources is feasible, but the only way to achieve this goal is by improving our understanding of ecological systems.' Many sustainability scientists, however, have recognized the limitations of this model. A central component of sustainability science is that research ought to be place-based (Kates *et al.* 2001; Turner *et al.* 2003a). This is in part because sustainable development efforts take place locally (Parris and Kates 2003). Place-based research allows scientists to work with potential users of knowledge to ensure that it is credible, salient and legitimate (Cash *et al.* 2003, 2006; Clark and Dickson 2003). As Clark *et al.* (2002: 24) note,

> for knowledge to be effective in advancing sustainable development goals, it must be widely viewed not only as reasonably likely to be true (i.e.,

'credible'), but also as relevant to decision makers' needs (i.e., 'salient') and as respectful and fair in its choice of issues to address, expertise to consider, and participants to engage (i.e., 'legitimate').

These characteristics are necessary to 'certify knowledge' (Clark *et al.* 2002). Sustainability scientists have proposed the concepts of boundary management and boundary organizations as crucial to negotiating the credibility, salience and legitimacy of knowledge between scientists and other stakeholders in order to ensure that scientific knowledge is used in decision making (Cash *et al.* 2003, 2006; Guston 1999, 2001; Kristjanson *et al.* 2009).

While these efforts offer a more nuanced interpretation of the relationship between knowledge and action, a tension remains as the assumptions of sustainability scientists are only slightly modified from those presented above:

1   science has not been producing the 'right' kind of knowledge; and
2   decision makers and society, more broadly, have not been utilizing the knowledge that science has produced.

According to this perspective, problems in the production and use of knowledge must be fixed before science can aid decision making. Science, up to this point, has not been addressing the questions to which society and decision makers need answers. 'Promoting the goal of sustainability requires the emergence and conduct of the new field of sustainability science' (Friiberg 2000: 1), which must be more applied and interdisciplinary in order to produce the knowledge that is required for decision making (Clark *et al.* 2002; Kates *et al.* 2001; Levin and Clark 2010). Decision makers and society, according to this assumption, have not been using the knowledge that science has produced because it is not perceived as credible, salient or legitimate. For example, as Pamela Matson explains, 'there has to be a pull' from decision makers or other stakeholders; they have to demand knowledge about certain issues (interview).

In this model, the role of science as knowledge provider has been ineffective because it has not been responding to demand or it is not being incorporated into decision making. In each of these cases, advancing societal action for sustainable outcomes is seen as requiring the production of more knowledge. This approach falls into what Sarewitz *et al.* (2010: 3) refer to as the *knowledge-first trap* 'where rational action is viewed as deriving from factually correct assessments of the causes of a problem.' The knowledge-first trap can lead to a spiral of endless research and technical debates (Collingridge and Reeve 1986; Nelson 2003; Sarewitz *et al.* 2010). Similarly, Collingridge and Reeve (1986: 5) argue that there is a fundamental mismatch 'between the needs of policy and the requirements for efficient research within science which forbids science any real influence on decision-making.'

For example, in 1980, transboundary acid rain policy was controversial in the United States. Congress created the National Acid Precipitation Assessment

Program (NAPAP) to reduce the uncertainties about the causes and effects of acid deposition before the nation committed itself to an acid reduction policy that was potentially costly (Herrick 2000). Although NAPAP created a wealth of scientific understanding about acid rain, many retrospective evaluations have criticized its failure to create an integrated and consistent policy recommendation for Congress. NAPAP failed to generate scientific knowledge that was useful for policy makers, since the causes and effects of acid rain are extremely complex. Studying them requires multiple scientific disciplines to synthesize incongruent methods, systems of knowledge and perspectives. Furthermore, NAPAP became preoccupied with fundamental research questions and moved away from its original, use-inspired orientation, thus eroding its potential value as an aide to policy making.

As discussed earlier, sustainability scientists both are motivated by pressing societal problems and aim to conduct research on fundamental questions about coupled system dynamics. Given the complexity and uncertainty inherent in sustainability issues, there is an understandable temptation to produce scientific knowledge in order to reduce uncertainty. In seeking to apply scientific knowledge to sustainability problems (Clark and Dickson 2003; Cash *et al.* 2003), sustainability scientists are treating wicked problems as if they were tame problems amenable to scientific analysis. A crucial step in navigating this tension is for sustainability scientists to begin to develop frameworks to differentiate between problems that may very well be tame and therefore amenable to technological fixes or the application of scientific knowledge, and those that are more wicked and for which narrow scientific and technical discourse will subvert the need for further ethical and political discussion.

While it may be the case that additional scientific knowledge is required to act on sustainability goals and advance sustainable practices, it may also be that there are a number of other, more proximate issues preventing action, such as technological capabilities and political debates. Without subjecting the link between scientific knowledge and beneficial societal outcomes to the same analytical rigor called for in addressing the challenges identified, the research that results may either be irrelevant to decision making or make such decisions even more difficult.

Scientizing sustainability

When dealing with wicked problems, the response is often to call for more research to reduce uncertainty and lay the foundation for policy action and decision making (Bocking 2004; Collingridge and Reeve 1986; Nelson 2003). As scientists move to focus on real world problems, they do so with their *weapon of choice* – scientific knowledge. As Clark (2010: 82) states,

> [l]ike 'agricultural science' and 'health science' before it, sustainability science is a field defined by the problems it addresses rather than the disciplines or methods it employs. Sustainability science then draws from – and seeks to advance – those aspects of our understanding of human systems, environ-

mental systems and their interactions that are useful for helping people achieve sustainability goals.

A brief examination of this analogy serves to highlight some of the tensions discussed in this chapter. Medical scientists perform research that aims to increase human health and decrease morbidity. Agricultural scientists seek to increase yields per acre and decrease input of resources per unit of output. However, how these goals are defined and problems solved in practice is far more complicated and contested.

For example, medical science has come under criticism for pursuing increases in life expectancy at the expense of quality of life (Fuchs 2010). There are many issues in the doctor–patient relationships in terms of defining health problems, treatment and positive outcomes (Teutsch 2003). These involve questions of values and how one wants to live one's life. Even the very notion of what is healthy can differ in various cultural contexts (Jamieson 1995). Furthermore, much of medical science, as measured by research funding, is far more concerned with end-of-life diseases such as heart disease and cancer, which are health problems in the developed world, than with chronic or acute ailments that develop earlier in life. This leaves diseases such as malaria and tuberculosis – having the largest impact on global human health, particularly in the developing world – with a paucity of funding and research. There is a misalignment between the diseases that contribute to the global burden of death and the dominant directions in medical research (Flory and Kitcher 2004). As Sarewitz (1996) reminds us, most research and development occurs in the developed world and is designed to address its specific problems (e.g. health of aging populations, space exploration, national security, consumption) and not those of the developing world (e.g. infant mortality, malaria, poverty, malnutrition).

As for agricultural science, there is little doubt that research and development has led to enormous increases in human well-being throughout the world. New technologies (e.g. high-yielding crop varietals), however, are not developed and deployed in context-free environments. Many efforts to increase crop yields, the Green Revolution in particular, have led to a mixed blessing at best as a result of a failure to adequately consider the social, economic and ecological context in which new crop varieties and information were being deployed. These artifacts of techno-science (Winner 1986) have shaped and been shaped by social and economic systems throughout the world as market and land tenure reforms were undertaken in an attempt to increase production and competitiveness (Moseley *et al.* 2010). Additionally, it is not clear that the lessons from such troubles have been learned, as illustrated in criticisms of renewed efforts for a second green revolution (this time focused on Africa) supported by the Rockefeller Foundation and Bill and Melinda Gates Foundation (e.g. Holt-Gimenez *et al.* 2006).

While these sciences may be shaped by the problems they address, the disciplines they employ also shape the definition of problems, how they are pursued and the potential solutions that they offer. A sustainability science modeled on these examples may fail to account for the difference and tensions between the context in which knowledge was initially developed and where and how it might be used. Both medical science and agricultural science are arenas in which the voices and knowledge of non-experts are largely unwelcome, with the exception of those instances where lay citizens have been able to adopt and change the language and concepts of the experts (see e.g. Epstein 1996). Techno-scientific changes in medicine have led to the 'medicalization' of society as scientific and technological interventions come not only to dominate efforts to improve human health but also to produce visions of what it means to be healthy (Clark and Dickson 2003; Conrad and Leiter 2004). Likewise, agricultural science has scientized agricultural practices and devalued traditional knowledge and practice (Howard 1994).

If the tensions discussed above are navigated poorly, sustainability science may (a) be limited in its ability to contribute to sustainability efforts, or (b) *scientize sustainability* via the epistemic authority of the analysis of coupled systems and thereby position itself to settle cultural and political disputes over sustainability. Appeals to scientific arguments and the expertise of sustainability scientists may mask or push aside important political and value debates about sustainability (Jasanoff 1996; Nowotny 1982; Sarewitz 1996). Scientific and technical debates act as proxies for what are in fact debates about values and the good life (Miller *et al.* 2011; Sarewitz 2004). Scientists at once acknowledge the importance and necessity of the normative dimensions of sustainability while establishing it as outside of their expertise. It is thereby divorced from their science, enhancing its perceived credibility as value-free. There is a short-circuiting of any and all questions about the nature of the bond between the sciences and society through the invocation of science (Latour 2004). Either outcome can be characterized as the result of 'faulty' boundary work; i.e. boundary work that preserves the epistemic authority and autonomy of science *at the expense of* beneficial societal outcomes. As Herbert Simon (1983: 97) notes,

> [w]hen an issue becomes highly controversial – when it is surrounded by uncertainties and conflicting values – then expertness is very hard to come by, and it is no longer so easy to legitimate the experts. In these circumstances we find that there are experts for affirmative and experts for the negative. We cannot settle such issues by turning them over to particular groups of experts.

Science can explore trade-offs between important social values and the possibilities of pursuing outcomes. Knowledge about coupled-system dynamics is surely necessary to manage them well over the long term. However, science does not present a certain, holistic picture of the world (Cartwright 1999; Dupré 1993). Nor is it value-free (Douglas 2009; Longino 1990, 2002). Just as sustainability science focuses on the coupled human–natural system in context, so too must the role of science be treated as contextual. Sustainability concerns the ability of communities to articulate and carry forward the social and natural values that are important to them and help to define their place (Norton 2005; O'Neill *et al.* 2008). Sustainability science may help inform and shape this process, but it should not dictate or define it. While sustainability scientists may not intend to do anything of the sort, as discussed through this chapter, the ways in which science can constrain debate and affect action can often be hidden and complex.

Rather than assuming that a lack of scientific knowledge is limiting decision-making capabilities, sustainability scientists might examine the occasions at which the level of scientific knowledge is regarded as a constraint on decision making. Sustainability scientists must begin to explore what solutions are possible and how they might be fostered and from there determine what (if any) scientific knowledge would be helpful. While scientific knowledge may indeed be necessary to take action on particular sustainability problems, others can likely be ameliorated without any major advance in scientific knowledge. There are social, cultural, political, normative and technological constraints that may be far more proximate to society's ability to pursue more sustainable outcomes.

Conclusion

As Simon (1983: 105) aptly observes in relation to decision making and social problems, 'scientific knowledge is not the Philosopher's Stone that is going to solve all these problems.' In fact, at least in the context of sustainability, scientific knowledge may inhibit the ability to solve certain problems by constraining debates, and lead to the assumption that more knowledge will generate better societal outcomes.

The point, however, is not to disparage current sustainability science efforts or argue that there is no hope for science to contribute to more sustainable social and environmental outcomes. There are several promising efforts in sustainability science and elsewhere that appear to be successfully navigating these tensions in their own ways. Fikret Berkes (2009a, 2009b), for example, is collaborating with indigenous groups in the Canadian Arctic to integrate traditional ecological knowledge with scientific ecology in community-based natural resource management. Researchers at the Dutch Research Institute for Transitions (DRIFT) work to develop transition arenas for a variety of sectors including health care, waste management, climate mitigation and urban development in which stakeholders can articulate goals and visions for more desirable outcomes and establish plans and policies to achieve them (Loorbach 2007; Loorbach and Rotmans 2009). Instead, the purpose, as I argue in Part II, is to maintain the capacity of sustainability to act as a platform from which to articulate and pursue democratic visions of natural and social well-being.

The tensions discussed in this chapter present a significant challenge to the practice of sustainability science, its usefulness to decision making and its institutional structure. Part II and the remaining chapters develop a more reflexive sustainability science that works to ensure the usefulness and relevance of knowledge in context. In part, how these tensions are navigated will determine the ability of sustainability science to encapsulate information in ways that are important to widely held social values and will help society pursue more sustainable outcomes.

References

Anderson, B. 1991. *Imagined communities: Reflections on the origin and spread of nationalism.* New York: Verso Press.

Appadurai, A. 1996. *Modernity at large: Cultural dimensions of globalization.* Minneapolis, MN: University of Minnesota Press.

Berkes, F. 2009a. Evolution of co-management: Role of knowledge generation, bridging organizations and social learning. *Journal of environmental management,* 90(5): 1692–1702.

Berkes, F. 2009b. Indigenous ways of knowing and the study of environmental change. Available at: www.sciencedirect.com/science/article/pii/S0301479708003587. [Accessed 13 August 2014.]

Bocking, S. 2004. *Nature's experts: Science, politics, and the environment.* New Brunswick, NJ: Rutgers University Press.

Bowker, G.C., and S.L. Star. 1999. *Sorting things out: Classification and its consequences.* Cambridge, MA: MIT Press.

Brown, S. 2009. The new deficit model. *Nature Nanotechnology* 4: 609–11.

Callon, M., Lascoumes, P., and Barthe, Y. 2009. *Acting in an uncertain world: An essay on technical democracy.* Cambridge, MA: MIT Press.

Carpenter, S.R., H.A. Mooney, J. Agard, D. Capistrano, R.S. DeFries, S. Diaz, T. Dietz, A.K. Duraiappah, A. Oteng-Yeboah, H.M. Pereira, C. Perrings, W.V. Reid, J. Sarukhan, R.J. Scholes, and A. Whyte. 2009. Science for managing ecosystem services: Beyond the Millennium Ecosystem Assessment. *Proceedings of the National Academy of Sciences* 106(5): 1305–12.

Cartwright, N. 1999. *The dappled world: A study of the boundaries of science.* Cambridge: Cambridge University Press.

Cash, D.W., W.C. Clark, F. Alcock, N.M. Dickson, N. Eckley, D.H. Guston, J. Jäger, and R.B. Mitchell. 2003. Knowledge systems for sustainable development. *Proceedings of the National Academy of Sciences of the United States of America* 100(14) (July 8): 8086–91.

Cash, D.W., J.C. Borck and A.G. Patt. 2006. Countering the loading-dock approach to linking science and decision making: Comparative analysis of El Niño/Southern Oscillation (ENSO) forecasting systems. *Science, Technology and Human Values* 31(4): 465–94.

Clark, W.C. 2007. Sustainability science: A room of its own. *Proceedings of the National Academy of Sciences* 104(6): 1737–1738.

Clark, W.C. 2010. Sustainable development and sustainability science. In report from Toward a Science of Sustainability Conference, Airlie Center, Warrenton, VA (2009).

Clark, W.C. and N.M. Dickson. 2003. Sustainability science: The emerging research program. *Proceedings of the National Academy of Sciences of the United States of America* 100(14) (July 8): 8059–61.

Clark, W.C., J. Buizer, D. Cash, R. Corell, N. Dickson, E. Dowdeswell, H. Doyle, G. Gallopín, G. Glaser, L. Goldfarb, A.K. Gupta, J.M. Hall, M. Hassan, A. Imevbore, M.M. Iwu, J. Jäger, C. Juma, R. Kates, D. Krömker, M. Kurushima, L. Lebel, Y.C. Lee, W. Lucht, A. Mabogunje, D. Malpede, P. Matson, B. Moldan, G. Montenegro, N. Nakicenovic, L.G. Ooi, T. O'Riordan, D. Pillay, T. Rosswall, J. Sarukhán, and J. Wakhungu. 2002. Science and technology for sustainable development: Consensus Report of the Mexico City Synthesis Workshop, 20–23 May 2002. Cambridge, MA: Initiative on Science and Technology for Sustainability.

Collingridge, D. and C. Reeve. 1986. *Science speaks to power: The role of experts in policy.* New York: St. Martin's Press.

Conrad, P. and V. Leiter. 2004. Medicalization, markets and consumers. *Journal of Health and Social Behavior* 45 (extra issue): 158–76.

Douglas, H.E. 2009. *Science, policy and the value-free ideal.* Pittsburgh, PA: University of Pittsburgh Press.

Dupré, J. 1993. *The disorder of things: Metaphysical foundations of the disunity of science.* Cambridge, MA: Harvard University Press.

Epstein, S. 1996. *Impure Science: AIDS, Activism, and the Politics of Knowledge.* Berkeley, CA: University of California Press.

Fischer, F. 2000. *Citizens, experts and the environment.* Durham, NC: Duke University Press.

Flory, J.H. and P. Kitcher. 2004. Global health and the scientific research agenda. *Philosophy and Public Affairs* 32(1): 36–65.

Friiberg Workshop Report. 2000. Sustainability science. Statement of the Friiberg Workshop on Sustainability Science, Friiberg, Sweden.

Fuchs, V.R. 2010. New priorities for future biomedical research. *New England Journal of Medicine* 363(8): 704–6.

Gieryn, T.F. 1999. *Cultural boundaries of science: Credibility on the line.* Chicago: University of Chicago Press.

Guston, D.H. 1999. Evaluating the first US consensus conference: The impact of the citizens' panel on telecommunications and the future of democracy. *Science, Technology and Human Values* 24(4): 451–82.

Guston, D.H. 2001. Boundary organizations in environmental policy and science: An introduction. *Science, Technology, & Human Values* 26(4): 399–408.

Hackett, E.J. 2005. Essential tensions: Identity, control, and risk in research. *Social Studies of Science* 35(5): 787–826.

Hardin, G. 1993. *Living within limits: ecology, economics, and population taboos.* Oxford: Oxford University Press.

Herrick, C. 2000. Predictive modeling of acid rain: Obstacles to generating useful information. In Daniel Sarewitz and Roger Pielke, Jr, (eds), *Prediction: Science, Decision Making, and the Future of Nature.* Washington DC: Island Press.

Holling, C.S. 2001. Understanding the complexity of economic, ecological and social systems. *Ecosystems* 4: 390–405.

Holt-Gimenez, E., M.A. Altieri, and P. Rosset. 2006. Ten reasons why the Rockefeller and the Bill and Melinda Gates Foundation's alliance for another green revolution will not solve the problems of poverty and hunger in Sub-Saharan Africa. Policy Brief No. 12, Institute for Food and Development Policy.

Howard, P. 1994. The confrontation of modern and traditional knowledge systems in development. *Canadian Journal of Communication* 19(2).

Jamieson, D. 1995. Ecosystem health: Some preventive medicine. *Environmental Values* 4(4): 333–44.

Jasanoff, S. 1990. *The fifth branch: Science advisers as policymakers.* Cambridge, MA: Harvard University Press.

Jasanoff, S. 1996. Science and norms in global environmental regimes. In Fen Osler Hampson and Judith Reppy, (eds), *Earthly Goods: Environmental Change and Social Justice,* pp 173–97. Ithaca, NY: Cornell University Press.

Jasanoff, S. 2004. Ordering knowledge, ordering society. In Sheila Jasanoff (ed.), *States of knowledge. The co-production of science and social order,* pp 13–45. New York: Routledge.

Jasanoff, S. 2005. *Designs on nature: Science and democracy in Europe and the United States.* Princeton, NJ: Princeton University Press.

Jasanoff, S. and B. Wynne. 1998. Science and decisionmaking. In Steve Rayner and Elizabeth Malone, (eds), *Human Choice and Climate Change, Vol. 1: The Societal Framework,* pp 1–87. Columbus, OH: Battelle Press.

Kates, R.W. 2001. Queries on the human use of the Earth. *Annual Review of Energy and Environment* 26: 1–26.

Kates, R.W., W.C. Clark, R. Corell, J.M. Hall, C.C. Jaeger, I. Lowe, J.J. McCarthy, H.J. Schellnhuber, B. Bolin, N.M. Dickson, S. Faucheux, G.C. Gallopin, A. Grübler, B. Huntley, J. Jäger, N.S. Jodha, R.E. Kasperson, A. Mabogunje, P. Matson, H. Mooney, B. Moore III, T. O'Riordan, and U. Svedin. 2001. Sustainability science. *Science* 292(5517): 641–2.

Komiyama, H. and K. Takeuchi. 2006. Sustainability science: Building a new discipline. *Sustainability Science* 1(1): 1–6.

Kristjanson, P., R.S. Reid, N. Dickson, W.C. Clark, D. Romney, R. Puskur, S. MacMillan, and D. Grace. 2009. Linking international agricultural research knowledge with action for sustainable development. *Proceedings of the National Academy of Sciences of the United States of America* 106(13): 5047–52.

Kuhn, T.S. 1977. *The essential tension: Selected studies in scientific tradition and change*. Chicago: University of Chicago Press.

Latour, B. 1987. *Science in action*. Cambridge, MA: Harvard University Press.

Latour, B. 1993. *We have never been modern*. Cambridge, MA: Harvard University Press.

Latour, B. 2004. *Politics of nature: How to bring the sciences into democracy*. Cambridge, MA: Harvard University Press.

Leshner, A. 2002. Science and sustainability. *Science* 297(5583): 897.

Levin, S.A. and W.C. Clark 2010. *Toward a science of sustainability*. Report from Toward a Science of Sustainability Conference, Airlie Center, Warrenton, VA, (2009).

Longino, H. 1990. *Science as social knowledge: Values and objectivity in scientific inquiry*. Princeton, NJ: Princeton University Press.

Longino, H. 2002. *The fate of knowledge*. Princeton, NJ: Princeton University Press.

Loorbach, D. 2007. *Transitions management: New mode of governance for sustainable development*. Utrecht, Netherlands: International Books.

Loorbach, D. and J. Rotmans. 2009. The practice of transitions management: Examples and lessons from four distinct cases. *Futures* 42(3): 237–46.

Lubchenco, J. 1998. Entering the century of the environment: A new social contract for science. *Science* 279(5350): 491.

Matson, P. 2009. The sustainability transition. *Issues in Science and Technology* Summer 2009: 39–42.

Mihelcic, J.R., J.C. Crittenden, M.J. Small, D.R. Shonnard, D.R. Hokanson, Q. Zhang, H. Chen, S.A. Sorby, V.U. James, J.W. Sutherland, and J.L. Schnoor. 2003. Sustainability science and engineering: The emergence of a new metadiscipline. *Environmental Science & Technology* 37(23): 5314–24.

Miller, C. 2005. New civic epistemologies of quantification: Making sense of indicators of local and global sustainability. *Science, Technology and Human Values* 30(3): 403–32.

Miller, C. 2008. Civic epistemologies: Constituting knowledge and order in political communities. *Sociology Compass* 2(6): 1896–1919.

Miller, T.R., T.D. Baird, C.M. Littlefield, G. Kofinas, F.S. Chapin III, and C.L. Redman. 2008. Epistemological pluralism: Reorganizing interdisciplinary research. *Ecology and Society* 13(2): 46. Available at: www.ecologyandsociety.org/vol13/iss2/art46/. [Accessed 31 July 2014.]

Miller, T.R., B.A. Minteer, and L. Malan. 2011. The new conservation debate: The view from practical ethics. *Biological Conservation* 144: 948–57.

Miller, T.R., and N.M. Neff. 2013. De-facto science policy in the making: How scientists shape science policy and why it matters (or, why STS and STP scholars should socialize). *Minerva* 51(3): 295–315.

Mooney, H.A., and O.E. Sala. 1993. Science and sustainable use. *Ecological Applications* 3: 564–566.

Moseley, W.G., J. Carney, and L. Becker. 2010. Neoliberal policy, rural livelihoods, and urban food security in West Africa: A comparative study of The Gambia, Côte d'Ivoire, and Mali. *Proceedings of the National Academy of Sciences of the United States of America* 107(13): 5774–9.

National Research Council. 1999. *Our common journey: A transition toward sustainability.* Washington, DC: National Academy Press.

Neff, M.W. 2011. What research should be done and why? Four competing visions among US ecologists. *Frontiers in Ecology and the Environment,* 9(8): 462–9.

Nelson, R.R. 1977. *The moon and the ghetto: An essay on public policy analysis.* The Fels Lectures on Public Policy Analysis. New York: W.W. Norton & Company.

Nelson, R.R. 2003. On the uneven evolution of human know-how. *Research Policy* 32: 909–22.

Norton, B.G. 2005. *Sustainability: A philosophy of adaptive ecosystem management.* Chicago: University of Chicago Press.

Nowotny, H. 1982. Experts in a participatory experiment – the Austrian debate on nuclear energy. *Bulletin of Science, Technology and Society* 2: 107–24.

O'Neill, J., A. Holland, and A. Light. 2008. *Environmental values.* New York: Routledge.

Palmer, M., E. Bernhardt, E. Chornesky, S. Collins, A. Dobson, C. Duke, B. Gold, R. Jacobson, S. Kingsland, R. Kranz, M. Mappin, M.L. Martinez, F. Micheli, J. Morse, M. Pace, M. Pascual, S. Palumbi, O.J. Reichman, A. Simons, A. Townsend, M. Turner. 2004. Ecology for a crowded planet. *Science* 304(5675): 1251–2.

Palmer, M., E. Bernhardt, E. Chornesky, S. Collins, A. Dobson, C. Duke, B. Gold, R. Jacobson, S. Kingsland, R. Kranz, M. Mappin, M.L. Martinez, F. Micheli, J. Morse, M. Pace, M. Pascual, S. Palumbi, O.J. Reichman, A. Simons, A. Townsend, M. Turner. 2005. Ecological science and sustainability for the 21st century. *Frontiers in Ecology and the Environment* 3(1): 4–11.

Parris, T.M. and R.W. Kates. 2003. Characterizing a sustainability transition: Goals, targets, trends, and driving forces. *Proceedings of the National Academy of Sciences* 100: 8068.

Pielke, R.A. Jr, D. Sarewitz, S. Rayner and G. Prins. 2007. Lifting the taboo on adaptation. *Nature* 445: 597–8.

Porter, T. 1995. *Trust in numbers: The pursuit of objectivity in science and public life.* Princeton, NJ: Princeton University Press.

Reid, W.V., D. Chen, L. Goldfarb, H. Hackman, Y.T. Lee, K. Mokhele, E. Ostrom, K. Raivio, J. Rockström, H.J. Schellnhuber, and A. Whyte. 2010. Earth system science for global sustainability: Grand challenges. *Science* 330: 916–17.

Robbins, P. 2001. Fixed categories in a portable landscape: The causes and consequences of land-cover categorization. *Environment and Planning A* 33(1): 161–80.

Sagoff, M. 2008. *The economy of the earth: Philosophy, law, and the environment,* 2nd edn. Cambridge: Cambridge University Press.

Sarewitz, D. 1996. *Frontiers of Illusion: Science, Technology, and the Politics of Progress.* Philadelphia, PA: Temple University Press.

Sarewitz, D. 2004. How science makes environmental controversies worse. *Environmental Science & Policy* 7(5): 385–403.

Sarewitz, D., D. Kriebel, R. Clapp, C. Crumbley, P. Hoppin, M. Jacobs, and J. Tickner. 2010. *The sustainable solutions agenda.* Consortium for Science, Policy and Outcomes and Lowell Center for Sustainable Production, Arizona State University and University of Massachusetts, Lowell.

Schellnhuber, H.J., P.J. Crutzen, W.C. Clark, M. Claussen, and H. Held (eds). 2004. *Earth System Analysis for Sustainability*. Cambridge, MA: MIT Press and Dahlem University Press.

Scott, J.C. 1998. *Seeing like a state: How certain schemes to improve the human condition have failed*. New Haven, CT: Yale University Press.

Shapin, S. and S. Schaffer. 1985. *Leviathan and the air-pump: Hobbes, Boyle, and the experimental life*. Princeton, NJ: Princeton University Press.

Shrader-Frechette, K.S., and E.D. McCoy. 1994. How the tail wags the dog: How value judgments determine ecological science. *Environmental Values*, 3(2): 107–20.

Simon, H.A. 1983. *Reason in human affairs*. Palo Alto, CA: Stanford University Press.

Smith, A., A. Stirling, F. Berkhout. 2005. The governance of sustainable socio-technical transitions. *Research Policy* 34: 1491–1510.

Smith, E. 2009. Imaginaries of development: The Rockefeller Foundation and rice research. *Science as Culture* 18(4): 451–82.

Sumi, A. 2007. On several issues regarding efforts toward a sustainable society. *Sustainability Science* 2(1): 67–76.

Teutsch, C. 2003. Patient–doctor communication. *Medical Clinics of North America* 87(5): 1115–45.

Thompson, P.B. 2010. *The agrarian vision: Sustainability and environmental ethics*. Lexington, KY: University of Kentucky Press.

Turner, B.L. II, P.A. Matson, J.J. McCarthy, R.W. Corell, L. Christensen, N. Eckley, G.K. Hovelsrud-Broda, J.X. Kasperson, R.E. Kasperson, A. Luers, M.L. Martello, S. Mathiesen, R. Naylor, C. Polsky, A. Pulsipher, A. Schiller, H. Selin, and N. Tyler. 2003a. Illustrating the coupled human–environment system for vulnerability analysis: Three case studies. *Proceedings of the National Academy of Sciences* 100(14): 8080–85.

Winner, L. 1986 *The whale and the reactor: A search for limits in an age of high technology*. Chicago: University of Chicago Press.

Worster, D. 1993. *The wealth of nature: Environmental history and the ecological imagination*. New York: Oxford University Press.

PART II
Reconstructing sustainability science

PART II

Reconstructing
sustainability science

5

RECLAIMING SUSTAINABILITY

Limits to knowledge

Part I explored the emergence of sustainability science, its empirical, normative and socio-political claims, and the tensions stemming from normative and epistemic positions in the field. This was an empirical and conceptual effort, drawing from STS, and laid the foundations for a reconstruction of sustainability science. Part II turns to a more prospective outlook, presenting a theoretical and conceptual argument for a reconstruction of sustainability science. This draws from the reconstructivist approach in STS discussed in Chapter 2 as well as from American pragmatist philosopher John Dewey's notion of reconstruction in philosophy.

As discussed in Chapters 3 and 4, efforts by scientists to contribute to sustainability often carry assumptions about the role of knowledge. However, there has been little done to first understand how visions of sustainability come to be articulated and then carve out a constructive role for science within that frame. Envisioning science without also envisioning sustainability and science's place within it makes much more difficult the task of constructing research agendas that might contribute to sustainability. Though sustainability science has certainly devoted its share of ink to defining sustainability, it has not done so in a way that makes clear how sustainability is being imagined, by whom and how science might contribute (or not). This is due in part to an insufficient appreciation of the social, moral and political dimensions of sustainability (Miller *et al.* 2009).

This tension between scientific and technical knowledge and social and ethical concerns is neither new nor unique to sustainability matters. In *Reconstruction in Philosophy*, John Dewey (1920) lamented the path of scientific and technological progress as ignoring deep political and moral concerns:

> Not only has the improvement in the method of knowing remained so far mainly limited to technical and economic matters, but this progress has brought with it serious new moral disturbances [war, capital and labor,

etc.]... These considerations indicate to us how undeveloped are our politics, how crude and primitive our education, how passive and inert our morals.

Similarly, environmental and sustainability issues have become increasingly driven by scientific and technical expertise (Feenberg 1999; Sclove 1994). Sustainability science needs a conceptual and normative effort that seeks to position science within a larger framework focused on the articulation of sustainability values and goals, and a deliberation over potential pathways to achieve them.

Why embark on yet another project that attempts to define, critique or salvage sustainability?[1] The concept and discourse of sustainability can act as a platform for our collectively imagined visions of natural and social well-being. As such, sustainability offers the possibility of challenging hegemonic notions of economic and technological progress and opening up alternative pathways (Leach et al. 2010; Stirling 2006). This broad normative scope is the source of both its discursive power and its popularity while also the source of many of its critiques (e.g. Worster 1993).

This chapter begins with a discussion of the limits of sustainability science given certain characteristics of sustainability problems as complex, uncertain and contested. This is not to simply critique the efforts of sustainability science. Instead, by understanding the epistemic and normative limits of science, we can begin to carve out a role for the field and the knowledge it produces that focuses on its ability to support deliberation over the meaning and pursuit of sustainability in context. This chapter concludes with a discussion of a conceptual framework for sustainability that will allow for a more action-oriented role for sustainability science as a science of design.

The limits of sustainability science

Sustainability science has largely focused on two objectives: Producing knowledge about human–environment interactions and linking that knowledge to action (Kates et al. 2001; Cash et al. 2003; Clark 2007; Friiberg 2000; Levin and Clark 2010). Sustainability science has been preoccupied with what can be referred to as the *knowledge-first approach*, the idea that more knowledge about underlying system dynamics will inform decisions and perhaps even compel action (Sarewitz et al. 2010). There are, however, severe limitations to this approach and to the scope for science to be of use in the contested, uncertain and value-laden context of sustainability.

While a lack of scientific knowledge can limit societal action in some cases, there are a myriad of social, political and technological issues and processes that are more proximate to the capacity of society to act more sustainably, even where additional scientific information is available (Collingridge and Reeve 1986; Miller et al. 2009; Nelson 1977, 2003). In fact, in an early critique of the role of science in sustainability issues, Ludwig et al. (1993) argue that the scientific community has helped to perpetuate the illusion that progress in science can lead to sustainability. This section examines the epistemic and normative limitations of sustainability science in order to gain insight into how they can be recognized and dealt with more effectively.

Epistemic limitations

Many sustainability problems present deep challenges to traditional scientific analyses and the role of science in society. Sustainability problems can often be classified as wicked problems – defined by high complexity, uncertainty, and contested social values (Funtowicz and Ravetz 1993; Ludwig 2001; Norton 2005; Rittel and Webber 1973). Traditional modes of inquiry cannot produce knowledge that is robust enough to withstand contested values and high complexity (Nowotny et al. 2001). In fact, such problems are often characterized by multiple conflicting and equally valid scientific and social interpretations (Collingridge and Reeve 1986; Sarewitz 2004).

This limitation, then, is not just epistemic, but socio-political. Epistemologically, the very idea that science can produce authoritative or reliable knowledge about complex and contested phenomena has been challenged (Funtowicz and Ravetz 1993; Nowotny et al. 2001). At the same time, the reliability and usefulness of scientific knowledge in society and in decision-making contexts has been called into question. The scientific norms (Merton 1973) and epistemic values (Douglas 2009) governing scientific practice have not evolved to deal with wicked problems and arenas in which the validity of scientific knowledge is challenged outside of the laboratory (Crow 2007; Funtowicz and Ravetz 1993; Gibbons 1999; Jasanoff 2010; Nowotny et al. 2001).

Science, in such cases, is unlikely to reduce uncertainty or provide a common foundation for social action. Stakeholders often demand predictive information about policy outcomes from scientists. Many scholars have criticized the reliance on predictive modeling to eliminate knowledge shortcomings when complex systems (such as the climate) are under scrutiny. Oreskes et al. (1994) have argued that verifying scientific models of complex systems is impossible owing to intractable epistemological limitations in understanding how a complex system's variables interact. Likewise, philosopher of science, Nancy Cartwright (1999) has argued that science tends not to produce grand, hierarchical systems of natural laws consistent between disciplines. Rather, the relationship between laws is tenuous and we should avoid thinking of science as creating a coherent and consistent picture of our world.

At best, science may be capable of informing decisions but never completely eliminate uncertainty in such complex systems; at worst, it may increase certain disputes and stall action. Such difficulties in the capacity of science to inform decision making often get attributed to social and political factors such as the public understanding of science or its politicization (Sarewitz 2010a; Wynne 1996). However, as Ludwig et al. (1993) argue, it is likely that science will never reach consensus regarding causal mechanisms and dynamics of complex, coupled human–natural systems.[2] More importantly, even if one were to grant that consensus in the scientific community is possible, meaningful social or political consensus on an understanding of an issue or a course of action is unlikely (Schwarz and Thompson 1990). This has as much to do with the epistemic practices of science and the wicked nature of sustainability problems, if not more, as it does with any perceived problems in the ability of decision makers to incorporate scientific knowledge into their decisions.

Scientists, decision makers and the broader public often perceive science as having privileged access to fact-based claims about the world (Jasanoff 2005; Latour 2004; Miller 2004). As a result, scientific knowledge and its perceived epistemic power can come to dominate alternative ways of knowing (Latour 2004; Scott 1998). Stephen Lansing's (1991) study of the disastrous (though well-intentioned) efforts by scientists and planners to reorganize farming practices in Bali, Indonesia highlights these issues.

During the Green Revolution, Balinese farmers were encouraged by planners, scientists and bureaucrats at the Bali Irrigation Project to abandon traditional cropping patterns and plant new, higher-yield, hybrid rice varieties as often as conditions permitted. Planners at the Project also sought to improve the perform-ance of the traditional irrigation systems through new construction and bureaucratic and scientific management. Before these changes brought about by the Green Revolution, Balinese farmers traditionally planned planting and harvesting through a complex social and technical process centered on a network of local water temples. Ultimately, these changes led to pest outbreaks and water shortages, particularly in the dry season, as scientists and planners attempted to plant a new round of resistant crops and develop new pesticides to stay ahead of the next potential rice pest. To the extent that social systems and the water temples entered into the analysis of the scientists and planners, it was largely in terms of the resistance of communities to the new technologies of the Green Revolution. Calls for return of the control over irrigation to water temples were perceived by the Bali Irrigation Project as religious conservatism and resistance to change. As one irrigation engineer responded, the farmers 'don't need a high priest, they need a hydrologist!' (Lansing 1991: 115).

Lansing (1991) poses what he views as a fundamental question – why was the functional role of water temples not a matter of common knowledge? He argues that the success of the water temples and traditional management practices made them invisible to scientists and planners studying them. Agriculture was viewed as a purely technical process. The invisibility of the water temples was also the result of the epistemic and disciplinary practices of the planners and scientists. The traditional management practices based on rituals performed at the water temples fell outside the boundaries of analysis for hydrologists, agricultural scientists and the like. These rites and rituals were not considered credible or legitimate by the planners, scientists and bureaucrats of the Bali Irrigation Project as they produced and utilized knowledge in different ways (Hacking 2004; Martello 2004; Miller 2008).

Scientific knowledge about coupled systems, their risks and vulnerabilities can shape discussion by highlighting certain aspects of the system and legitimizing some knowledge claims over others. As Norton (2002: 22) notes, in such contexts where interests vie to affect policy and management outcomes, 'the relevant language cannot be the specialized languages of either a narrow, disciplinary science or of a narrow theory about what is meant by a small subset of the society.' While the efforts of sustainability scientists may not be as heavy-handed as the Balinese Irrigation Project, the scientists still must be aware of the ways in which their epistemic viewpoint can be both limited, resulting in certain factors becoming invisible, and constrain discourse and alternative understandings of sustainability, through its perceived power as value-free.

Interdisciplinary research has emerged as a core characteristic of sustainability science and similar applied efforts in an attempt to overcome the fragmented and partial picture of problems presented by isolated disciplines. Many adherents of an interdisciplinary approach argue that it will provide a more complete and holistic account of the system or problem under investigation. For example if, in addition to engineers, hydrologists, and agricultural sciences, social scientists and humanists had been included in the Bali Irrigation Project, the importance of the water temple institution might have been realized and taken into account. While an interdisciplinary approach can provide insights that may not have been possible from a strict disciplinary perspective, the quest for a more holistic picture of reality does not overcome the epistemic limitations of sustainability science (Sarewitz 2012). There still may be a variety of valid interpretations (Miller *et al.* 2008) and there are limits to what we can know, particularly in the face of complexity (Crow 2007; Stirling 2010).

To the extent that sustainability problems become settled, this will be through a social and political effort of which science is but a part. Sustainability and its problems cut across disciplinary boundaries and defy both problem definition and easy solutions; they challenge not just the analytical tools and approaches of scientists but the use of scientific knowledge in society. As Nelson (2003) notes, this is not a comment on the quality of research in fields such as sustainability science. Instead, it is related to limitations on the scope of scientific research to advance action in areas that are highly social and contextual.

Normative limitations

As discussed in Chapter 4, science can at once reveal issues that are of normative concern *and* constrain what is considered appropriate dialogue on the very same issues (Bocking 2004; Latour 2004; Longino 2002). How sustainability science navigates this tension can either empower or limit the ability of communities to articulate visions and goals for sustainability.

Most sustainability scientists acknowledge that they are indeed motivated by the problems and concerns of sustainability (Chapin *et al.* 2009). As F. (Terry) Stuart Chapin III noted in an interview, '[i]t [sustainability] may be more of a calling on ethics and a sense of responsibility to the planet, a sense of responsibility to future generations.' However, the core of the sustainability science agenda is fundamental research into the dynamics of coupled human–natural systems (Carpenter et al. 2009; Levin and Clark 2010; Matson 2009). Values, many scientists argue, are better dealt with by decision makers and other stakeholders. Citing the Brundtland Report (WCED 1987) or the National Research Council (1999) definition of the term, sustainability scientists embrace the values of sustainability, while at the same time maintaining a distance from such values by focusing on fundamental research. The role of the sustainability scientists is to supply knowledge that is perceived as credible, salient and legitimate and will inform decision making in a value-free manner (Cash et al. 2003; Clark et al. 2002). In so doing, sustainability science is able to maintain an epistemic core of fundamental research that is value-free (Douglas 2009; Gieryn 1983, 1995).

For all this, key concepts in sustainability science such as risk and vulnerability (Turner et al. 2003a,b), tipping points (Scheffer et al. 2009; Schellnhuber 2009), planetary boundaries (Rockström et al. 2009), and even defining the boundaries and interactions between human and natural systems are suffused with values. The act of defining aspects of a wicked problem for scientific inquiry is inherently value-laden, with implications for democratic problem-solving and the pursuit of potential solutions (Fischer 2000; Jasanoff 2007; Latour 2004).

For example, the climate science community has predicted that a doubling of atmospheric carbon dioxide concentrations from pre-industrialization levels will result in a 1.5°C to 4.5°C increase in the global average atmospheric temperature (Rayner 2000; van der Sluijs et al. 1998). Beyond this temperature threshold, catastrophic climatic events await. Nonetheless, the estimated temperature increase as a result of a doubling in CO_2 has barely changed since Arrhenius's work on the greenhouse effect in the late nineteenth century (van der Sluijs et al. 1998). This is despite significant advances and investments in global circulation models and climate science more generally. Research has focused on classifying the uncertainties around this prediction and attempting to specify potential consequences (Rayner 2000). This has come at the expense of an expanded discussion that includes *local* (rather than just global) risks and vulnerabilities, adaption and technological solutions (Hulme et al. 2009; Pielke, Jr. et al. 2007; Rayner and Malone 1997). The scientific framing of climate change as a *global* problem that science can appropriately manage is also a social and political framing that has made it more difficult to introduce alternative understandings and normative concerns into the discussion (Sarewitz and Pielke, Jr. 2007; Jasanoff 2001; Miller 2004).[3]

The epistemic power of science, especially when presented or perceived as value-free, can come to dominate normative and political concerns (Douglas 2009; Latour 2004). The normative limitation of sustainability science is in its potential failure to recognize the degree to which supposedly value-free science is in fact value-laden and how scientific analyses can influence necessary and important political debates in society in complex ways. The challenge is to construct a science that is able to convey important information in a way that allows a plurality of values and understandings to emerge.

Each of the limitations discussed above is maintained and reinforced by the institutional structure of science. Scientists are incentivized through their training and evaluation to advance knowledge in their home discipline. Many of the activities that might be necessary to contribute to such outcomes, including inter-disciplinary or participatory research, are challenging, time-consuming and rarely rewarded within the academy (Miller *et al.* 2008, 2011; Roux *et al.* 2006; Rowe 2007). Any change in the research agenda for sustainability science must be pursued in conjunction with institutional change.

Conclusion

A sustainability transition, however defined, will be a social, cultural and political process (Miller *et al.*, 2009). The scientific community has certainly recognized as much (Kates *et al.*, 2001), but has not adequately considered precisely how science is to fit into this process. If sustainability science is to work towards providing knowledge for a sustainability transition, the science cannot be considered as separate from the social, ethical and political dimensions. This is because of the structure of disciplines and the ways science interrogates the world and of the ways in which we have fragmented the tasks of science, politics and society.

Sustainability up to this point has done admirably well in defining what Toulmin (1990) calls our 'horizons of expectations.' Horizons of expectations frame possible futures. Popular definitions of sustainability, like those put forth by Brundtland (WCED 1987) and the NRC (1999), formulated reasonable horizons of expect-ations or a desirable space in which humanity would like to exist; i.e. society should develop in a way that limits negative impacts on (or even seeks positive interactions with) ecological support systems, reduces social injustices including hunger and poverty, and takes a long-term perspective. What is missing is how to navigate within these horizons and carve out more specific future pathways.

Futures, notes Toulmin (1990: 2), 'do not simply happen of *themselves*, but can be *made to* happen, if we meanwhile adopt wise attitudes and policies.' Toulmin continues:

> A well formulated approach to the future – a realistic range of available futuribles, within reasonable horizons of expectation – does not depend on finding ways to quantify and extrapolate current trends: that we may leave to enthusiastic weather forecasters, stock exchange chartists, or econometrists. Rather, the questions are, 'What intellectual posture should we adopt in con-fronting the future? What eye can we develop for significant aspects of the years ahead? And what capacity do we have to change our ideas about available futures?' Those who refuse to think coherently about the future, correspondingly, only expose themselves to worse, leaving the field clear to unrealistic, irrational prophets.

This is fruitful ground for development a schematic definition of sustainability that allows for a more constructive and open role for science. *Sustainability is a way of articulating visions of human and natural well-being and devising strategies to pursue those visions.* This definition is more schematic in nature rather than setting specific goals or indicators. It allows the moral and ethical vision of well-being to reside alongside the social, political, scientific and technological issue of how we might actually bring it to fruition. Science alone cannot *make* a future to happen; however, it can help us identify implications of such futures and their plausibility. Science is necessary to help get a sense of possible futures and frame our horizons. Sustainability science is well positioned to fit in this role.

In the following chapter, I develop a sustainability science of design that is concerned with the pursuit of sustainable futures, as opposed to simply understanding problems in the past and present.

Notes

1   See, for instance, Davison 2000, Edwards 2005, Parr 2009, Moore 2010, Thompson 2010.

2   The perceived scientific consensus on climate change may seem to counter this claim. However, the consensus on the basic mechanisms behind climate change has not translated into concerted social action. Furthermore, as research in science studies has shown, this supposed consensus is fragile and hides significant and legitimate differences. The ability to achieve consensus is driven by social norms and processes, as well as institutional configurations (Jasanoff and Wynne 1998; Miller 2004; Schackley 2001; van der Sluijs *et al.* 1998). In addition, as recent events such as 'Climate Gate' have shown, such consensus is liable to be reopened and challenged, providing a glimpse into the social, political and normative dimensions of scientific knowledge-making. This has as much (if not more) to do with social norms of scientific communities and institutions and political consensus (or lack thereof) as it does with the strength of scientific findings (Hulme 2010; Jasanoff 2010).

3   Normative and ethical critiques of climate change-normative analyses have focused primarily on issues related to the responsibility for greenhouse gas emissions and a fair and just allocation of future emissions (Jamieson 1992; Brown 2002; Gardiner 2004). Largely missing from this discussion is an intra-generationally more important question of how to help those currently vulnerable to climate and weather variability adapt in fair and just ways.

References

Bocking, S. 2004. *Nature's experts: Science, politics, and the environment.* New Brunswick, NJ: Rutgers University Press.

Brown, D. 2002. *American heat: Ethical problems with the United Statesresponse to global warming.* Lanham, MD: Rowman and Littlefield.

Carpenter, S.R., H.A. Mooney, J. Agard, D. Capistrano, R.S. DeFries, S. Diaz, T. Dietz, A.K. Duraiappah, A. Oteng-Yeboah, H.M. Pereira, C. Perrings, W.V. Reid, J. Sarukhan, R.J. Scholes, and A. Whyte. 2009. Science for managing ecosystem services: Beyond the Millennium Ecosystem Assessment. *Proceedings of the National Academy of Sciences* 106(5): 1305–12.

Cartwright, N. 1999. *The dappled world: A study of the boundaries of science.* Cambridge: Cambridge University Press.

Cash, D.W., W.C. Clark, F. Alcock, N.M. Dickson, N. Eckley, D.H. Guston, J. Jäger, and R.B. Mitchell. 2003. Knowledge systems for sustainable development. *Proceedings of the National Academy of Sciences of the United States of America* 100(14): 8086–91.

Chapin, F. Stuart III, S.R. Carpenter, G.P. Kofinas, C. Folke, N. Abel, W.C. Clark, P. Olsson, D.M. Stafford Smith, B. Walker, O.R. Young, F. Berkes, R. Biggs, J.M. Grove, R.L. Naylor, E. Pinkerton, W. Steffen, and F.J. Swanson. 2009. Ecosystem stewardship: Sustainability strategies for a rapidly changing planet. *Trends in Ecology and Evolution* 25(4): 241–9.

Clark, W.C. 2007. Sustainability science: A room of its own. *Proceedings of the National Academy of Sciences* 104(6): 1737–8.

Clark, W.C., J. Buizer, D. Cash, R. Corell, N. Dickson, E. Dowdeswell, H. Doyle, G. Gallopín, G. Glaser, L. Goldfarb, A.K. Gupta, J.M. Hall, M. Hassan, A. Imevbore, M.M. Iwu, J. Jäger, C. Juma, R. Kates, D. Krömker, M. Kurushima, L. Lebel, Y.C. Lee, W. Lucht, A. Mabogunje, D. Malpede, P. Matson, B. Moldan, G. Montenegro, N. Nakicenovic, L.G. Ooi, T. O'Riordan, D. Pillay, T. Rosswall, J. Sarukhán, and J. Wakhungu. 2002. Science and technology for sustainable development: Consensus Report of the Mexico City Synthesis Workshop, 20–23 May 2002. Cambridge, MA: Initiative on Science and Technology for Sustainability.

Collingridge, D. and C. Reeve. 1986. *Science speaks to power: The role of experts in policy.* New York: St Martin's Press.

Crow, M.M. 2007. None dare call it hubris: The limits of knowledge. *Issues in Science and Technology*, Winter: 1–4.

Davison, A. 2000. *Technology and the contested meanings of sustainability.* Albany, NY: State University of New York Press.

Dewey, J. 1920. *Reconstruction in philosophy.* In Jo Ann Boydston, (ed.), *The middle works, vol. 12.* Carbondale, IL: Southern Illinois University Press.

Douglas, H.E. 2009. *Science, policy and the value-free ideal.* Pittsburgh, PA: University of Pittsburgh Press.

Edwards, A.R. and D.W. Orr 2005. *The Sustainability Revolution: Portrait of a Paradigm Shift.* Gabriola Island, BC, Canada: New Society Publishers.

Feenberg, A. 1999. *Questioning technology.* Routledge: New York.

Fischer, F. 2000. *Citizens, experts and the environment.* Durham, NC: Duke University Press.

Friiberg Workshop Report. 2000. Sustainability science. Statement of the Friiberg Workshop on Sustainability Science, Friiberg, Sweden.

Funtowicz, S.O., and J.R. Ravetz. 1993. Science for the post-normal age. *Futures* 25(7): 739–55.

Gardiner, S. 2004. Ethics and global climate change. *Ethics* 114: 555–600.

Gibbons, M. 1999. Science's new social contract with society. *Nature* 402: C81.

Gieryn, T.F. 1983. Boundary-work and the demarcation of science from non-science: Trains and interests in professional interests of scientists. *American Sociological Review* 48: 781–95.

Gieryn, T.F. 1995. Boundaries of science. In *Handbook of science and technology studies.* Sheila Jasanoff, Gerald E. Markle, James C. Petersen, and Trevor Pinch, eds. Rev. edn. Thousand Oaks, CA: Sage Publications.

Hacking, I. 2004. *Historical Ontology.* Cambridge, MA: Harvard University Press.

Hulme, M. 2010. Problems with making global kinds of knowledge. *Global Environmental Change* 20: 558–64.

Hulme, M., R.A. Pielke, Jr, and S. Dessai. 2009. Keeping prediction in perspective. *Nature Reports Climate Change* 3: 126–7.

Jamieson, D. 1992. Ethics, public policy, and global warming. *Science, Technology, and Human Values* 17(2): 139–53.

Jasanoff, S. 2001. Image and imagination: The formation of global environmental consciousness. In Paul Edwards and Clark Miller, (eds), *Changing the Atmosphere: Expert Knowledge and Environmental Governance*. Cambridge, MA: MIT Press.

Jasanoff, S. 2005. *Designs on nature: Science and democracy in Europe and the United States*. Princeton, NJ: Princeton University Press.

Jasanoff, S. 2007. Technologies of humility. *Nature* 450: 33.

Jasanoff, S. 2010. Testing time for climate science. *Science* 328(5979): 695–6.

Jasanoff, S. and B. Wynne. 1998. Science and decisionmaking. In Steve Rayner and Elizabeth Malone, (eds), *Human Choice and Climate Change, Vol. 1: The Societal Framework*. Columbus, OH: Battelle Press.

Kates, R.W., W.C. Clark, R. Corell, J.M. Hall, C.C. Jaeger, I. Lowe, J.J. McCarthy, H.J. Schellnhuber, B. Bolin, N.M. Dickson, S. Faucheux, G.C. Gallopin, A. Grübler, B. Huntley, J. Jäger, N.S. Jodha, R.E. Kasperson, A. Mabogunje, P. Matson, H. Mooney, B. Moore III, T. O'Riordan, and U. Svedin. 2001. Sustainability science. *Science* 292(5517): 641–2.

Lansing, J.S. 1991. *Priests and programmers: Technologies of power in the engineered landscape of Bali*. Princeton, NJ: Princeton University Press.

Latour, B. 2004. *Politics of nature: How to bring the sciences into democracy*. Cambridge, MA: Harvard University Press.

Leach, M., I. Scoones, and A. Stirling (eds), 2010. *Dynamic Sustainabilities: Technology, Environment, Social Justice (Pathways to Sustainability)*. London, New York: EarthScan.

Levin, S.A. and W.C. Clark 2010. *Toward a science of sustainability*. Report from Toward a Science of Sustainability Conference, Airlie Center, Warrenton, VA (2009).

Longino, H. 2002. *The fate of knowledge*. Princeton, NJ: Princeton University Press.

Ludwig, D. 2001. The era of management is over. *Ecosystems* 4(8): 758–64.

Ludwig, D., R. Hilborn and C. Walters. 1993. Uncertainty, resource exploitation, and conservation: Lessons from history. *Ecological Applications* 3(4): 548–9.

Martello, M.L. 2004. Negotiating global nature and local culture: The case of Makah whaling. In Sheila Jasanoff and Marybeth Long Martello, (eds), *Earthly politics: local and global environmental governance*. Cambridge, MA: MIT Press.

Matson, P. 2009. The sustainability transition. *Issues in Science and Technology* Summer 2009: 39–42.

Merton, R.K. 1973. *The sociology of science*. Chicago: University of Chicago Press.

Miller, C. 2004. Resisting empire: Globalism, relocation, relocalization, and the politics of knowledge. In Sheila Jasanoff and Marybeth Long Martello, (eds), *Earthly politics: Local and global environmental governance*. Cambridge, MA: MIT Press.

Miller, C. 2008. Civic epistemologies: Constituting knowledge and order in political communities. *Sociology Compass* 2(6): 1896–1919.

Miller, C., D. Sarewitz and A. Light. 2009. *Science, technology and sustainability: Building a research agenda*. Report National Science Foundation supported workshop, September 8–9, 2008.

Miller, T.R., T.D. Baird, C.M. Littlefield, G. Kofinas, F.S. Chapin III, and C.L. Redman. 2008. Epistemological pluralism: Reorganizing interdisciplinary research. *Ecology and Society* 13(2): 46. Available at: www.ecologyandsociety.org/vol13/iss2/art46/. [Accessed 1 August 2014.]

Miller, T.R., B.A. Minteer, and L. Malan. 2011. The new conservation debate: The view from practical ethics. *Biological Conservation* 144: 948–57.

Moore, S.A. (ed.) 2010. *Pragmatic Sustainability: Theoretical and Practical Tools*. London: Routledge.

National Research Council. 1999. *Our common journey: A transition toward sustainability.* Washington, DC: National Academy Press.

Nelson, R.R. 1977. *The moon and the ghetto: An essay on public policy analysis.* The Fels Lectures on Public Policy Analysis. New York: W.W. Norton & Company.

Nelson, R.R. 2003. On the uneven evolution of human know-how. *Research Policy* 32: 909–22.

Norton, B.G. 2002. Democracy and environmentalism: Foundations and justifications in environmental policy. In Ben A. Minteer and Bob Pepperman Taylor, (eds), *Democracy and the claims of nature: Critical perspectives for a new century.* Lanham, MD: Rowman and Littlefield.

Norton, B.G. 2005. *Sustainability: A philosophy of adaptive ecosystem management.* Chicago: University of Chicago Press.

Nowotny, H., P. Scott and M. Gibbons. 2001. *Re-thinking science: Knowledge and the public in an age of uncertainty.* Malden, MA: Polity.

Oreskes, N., K. Shrader-Frechette, and K. Belitz. 1994. Verification, validation, and confirmation of numerical models in the earth sciences. *Science* 263(5147): 641–6.

Parr, A. 2009. *Hijacking Sustainability.* Cambridge, MA: MIT Press.

Pielke, R.A. Jr, D. Sarewitz, S. Rayner and G. Prins. 2007. Lifting the taboo on adaptation. *Nature* 445: 597–8.

Rayner, S. 2000. Prediction and other approaches to climate change. In Daniel Sarewitz and Roger Pielke, Jr., (eds), *Prediction: Science, Decision Making, and the Future of Nature.* Washington DC: Island Press.

Rayner, S. and E. Malone. 1997. Zen and the art of climate maintenance. *Nature* 390: 332–4.

Rittel, H.W.J. and M.M. Webber. 1973. Dilemmas in a general theory of planning. *Policy Sciences* 4: 155–69.

Rockström, J., W. Steffen, K. Noone, Å. Persson, F.S. Chapin III, E.F. Lambin, T.M. Lenton, M. Scheffer, C. Folke, H. Joachim Schellnhuber, B. Nykvist, C.A. de Wit, T. Hughes, S. van der Leeuw, H. Rodhe, S. Sörlin, P.K. Snyder, R. Costanza, U. Svedin, M. Falkenmark, L. Karlberg, R.W. Corell, V.J. Fabry, J. Hansen, B. Walker, D. Liverman, K. Richardson, P. Crutzen, and J.A. Foley. 2009. A safe operating space for humanity. *Nature* 461: 472–5.

Roux, D.J., K.H. Rogers, H.C. Biggs, P.J. Ashton, and A. Sergeant. 2006. Bridging the science–management divide: Moving from unidirectional knowledge transfer to knowledge interfacing and sharing. *Ecology and Society* 11(1): 4. Available at: www.ecologyandsociety.org/vol11/iss1/art4. [Accessed 1 August 2014.]

Rowe, D. 2007. Education for a sustainable future. *Science* 317: 323–4.

Sarewitz, D. 2004. How science makes environmental controversies worse. *Environmental Science & Policy* 7(5): 385–403.

Sarewitz, D. 2010a. Worldview: Politicize me. *Nature* 467: 26.

Sarewitz, D. 2010b. Against holism. In Robert Frodeman, Julie Thompson Klein, Carl Mitcham, (eds), *The Oxford Handbook of Interdisciplinarity,* Oxford: Oxford University Press.

Sarewitz, D. and R.A. Pielke, Jr. 2007. The neglected heart of science policy: Reconciling supply of and demand for science. *Environmental Science and Policy* 10(1): 5–16.

Sarewitz, D., D. Kriebel, R. Clapp, C. Crumbley, and J. Tickner. 2012. The sustainable solutions agenda. *New Solutions,* 22(2): 139–51.

Scheffer, M., J. Bascompte, W.A. Brock, V. Brovkin, S.R. Carpenter, V. Dakos, H. Held, E.H. van Nes, M. Rietkerk, and G. Sugihara. 2009. Early-warning signs for critical transitions. *Nature* 461: 53–9.

Schellnhuber, H.J. 2009. Tipping elements in Earth systems special feature: Tipping elements in the Earth system. *Proceedings of the National Academy of Sciences* 106(49): 20561–3.

Schwarz, M. and M. Thompson. 1990. *Divided we stand: Redefining politics, technology and social choice*. Philadelphia, PA: University of Pennsylvania Press.

Sclove, R. 1994. *Democracy and Technology*. New York: The Guilford Press.

Scott, J.C. 1998. *Seeing like a state: How certain schemes to improve the human condition have failed*. New Haven, CT: Yale University Press.

Shackley, S. 2001. Epistemic lifestyles in climate change modeling. In Clark A. Miller and Paul N. Edwards (eds), *Changing the Atmosphere: Expert Knowledge and Environmental Governance*. Cambridge, MA: MIT Press.

Stirling, A. 2006. Precaution, foresight, and sustainability: Reflection and reflexivity in the governance of science and technology. In J.P. Voß, D. Bauknecht, R. Kemp, (eds), *Reflexive Governance for Sustainable Development*. Cheltenham, UK: Edward Elgar.

Stirling, A. 2010. Keep it complex. *Nature* 468: 1029–31.

Thompson, P.B. 2010. *The agrarian vision: Sustainability and environmental ethics*. Lexington, KY: University of Kentucky Press.

Toulmin, S. 1990. *Cosmopolis: The Hidden Agenda of Modernity*. Chicago: University of Chicago Press.

Turner, B.L. II, P.A. Matson, J.J. McCarthy, R.W. Corell, L. Christensen, N. Eckley, G.K. Hovelsrud-Broda, J.X. Kasperson, R.E. Kasperson, A. Luers, M.L. Martello, S. Mathiesen, R. Naylor, C. Polsky, A. Pulsipher, A. Schiller, H. Selin, and N. Tyler. 2003a. Illustrating the coupled human–environment system for vulnerability analysis: Three case studies. *Proceedings of the National Academy of Sciences* 100(14): 8080–85.

Turner, B.L. II, R.E. Kasperson, P.A. Matson, J.J. McCarthy, R.W. Corell, L. Christensen, N. Eckley, J.X. Kasperson, A. Luers, M.L. Martello, C. Polsky, A. Pulsipher, and A. Schiller. 2003b. A framework for vulnerability analysis in sustainability science. *Proceedings of the National Academy of Sciences* 100(14): 8074–9.

van der Sluijs, J., J. van Eijndhoven, S. Shakley, and B. Wynne. 1998. Anchoring devices in science for policy: The case of consensus around climate sensitivity. *Social Studies of Science* 28(2): 291–323.

World Commission on Environment and Development (WCED). 1987. *Our common future*. New York: Oxford University Press.

Worster, D. 1993. *The wealth of nature: Environmental history and the ecological imagination*. New York: Oxford University Press.

Wynne, B. 1996. Misunderstood misunderstandings: Social identities and the public uptake of science. In Alan Irwin and Brian Wynne, (eds), *Misunderstanding Science?: The Public Reconstruction of Science and Technology*. Cambridge: Cambridge University Press.

6

SUSTAINABILITY AS A SCIENCE OF DESIGN

Angelus Novus

Upon viewing Paul Klee's *Angelus Novus* at a gallery exhibition, Walter Benjamin was deeply affected. In *On the Concept of History* (1940), Benjamin describes this encounter:

> There is a painting by Klee called Angelus Novus. An angel is depicted there who looks as though he were about to distance himself from something which he is staring at. His eyes are opened wide, his mouth stands open and his wings are outstretched. The Angel of History must look just so. His face is turned towards the past. Where we see the appearance of a chain of events, he sees one single catastrophe, which unceasingly piles rubble on top of rubble and hurls it before his feet. He would like to pause for a moment so fair, to awaken the dead and to piece together what has been smashed. But a storm is blowing from Paradise, it has caught itself up in his wings and is so strong that the Angel can no longer close them. The storm drives him irresistibly into the future, to which his back is turned, while the rubble-heap before him grows sky-high. That which we call progress, is this storm.

Science, in many respects, provides us with the viewpoint of the Angel looking to the past for knowledge about our present and future. Scientific knowledge has been, and continues to be, an incredibly powerful tool for society to understand our world. In Beck's (1992) risk society, this increasingly entails understanding the myriad social and environmental problems that our use of science and technology has generated. Even efforts like sustainability science, concerned with use-inspired research, are but attempting to understand 'how the rubble-heap before' us is being built up; yet this understanding of sustainability problems is not enough.

Benjamin sees the Angel being driven 'irresistibly into the future, to which his back is turned.' So, too, has sustainability science, and science more broadly, had its gaze focused on the past, attempting to understand underlying problem dynamics. We hope this improved understanding will help us act in a future to which our backs are turned. Can sustainability science turn, and find a pathway into the future, instead of being propelled into it? Put differently, how can science shift from identifying and describing problems in the ecophysical realm to contributing to potential solutions in social and political realms? This chapter takes up this question.

A science of design

This chapter repositions sustainability science as a 'science of design' – that is, a science of what *ought* to be in order to achieve certain goals, rather than a science of what *is*. This follows Nobel Laureate Herbert Simon's (1996) notion of the artificial sciences as sciences of design. The artificial sciences are concerned with how things 'ought to be in order to *attain goals* and to *function*' (Simon 1996: 4–5). Here, I also utilize John Dewey's (1920, 1938) pragmatism which serves to ground sustainability science in lived experience with advances in inquiry measured by progress in achieving goals. The knowledge produced by sustainability should be helpful in bringing desired outcomes to fruition. Following Simon and Dewey, this chapter develops a more pragmatic sustainability science that is evaluated on its ability to frame sustainability problems and solutions in ways that make them amenable to democratic social action.

It is not enough for sustainability science to focus on the analysis of the system dynamics underlying certain problems; it must move toward research that is focused on the design of solutions. Following the sustainable solutions agenda of Sarewitz *et al.* (2010), sustainability science must not be limited to research into the 'problem space,' but also be concerned with the space in which solutions are formulated and implemented, the 'solution space.' This is not say that sustainability science should only focus on the development of 'one-size-fits-all' solutions. Rather, the point is to focus on the context in which solutions might be developed and deployed, exploring how scientific knowledge or other tools might help in advancing desirable outcomes.

Sustainability is a forward-looking, future-oriented concept that provides a conceptual platform for communities to articulate visions of social and natural well-being. Ironically, it is also partially backward-looking in that what is being sustained is a set of goods and values that have come to define a community over time. The mission of sustainability science should be to help bring such visions to fruition. Accordingly, I develop two core objectives for this reconstructed field: (1) to understand and contribute to the design of sustainable solutions; and (2) to promote reasoning and deliberation over the meanings, goals and pursuit of sustainability.

Sustainability science, however, is ill-equipped to meet these objectives. This is not a result of an obvious flaw in how sustainability scientists have constructed their research agendas. On the contrary, part of the reason that the field has attracted attention is its ability to speak to a major gap in scientific research – interdisciplinary approaches to human–environment interactions and the claim that the knowledge gained from such research will support decision making. This approach, however, falls short on fostering sustainable outcomes as a result of certain epistemic and normative limitations as well as a research agenda limited to addressing fundamental questions about coupled human–natural systems.

Objectives for a science of design

Sustainability presents a unique set of epistemic, normative and institutional challenges to science and its ability to contribute to positive, more sustainable social and environmental outcomes. The core question now facing sustainability science is: How can sustainability science shift from identifying problems in the biophysical realm to contributing to the pursuit of solutions in the social and political realm? This question requires scientists to face another that is deeper yet: To what extent and in what ways is science necessary to advance sustainable outcomes? In order for sustainability science to address these questions, changes are necessary in the way sustainability is conceptualized, how sustainability science investigates problems and their potential solutions, and in the way we act to address them (Mitchell 2009).

In this section, I utilize Simon's notion of a science of design supported by Dewey's pragmatic philosophy to reconstruct sustainability science as a more pragmatic mode of inquiry focused on problem solving and the design of solutions. Following Dewey's (1920) own reconstructive project, I consider how science can best contribute to sustainability and propose two core objectives for the field that heretofore have been either underdeveloped in or entirely absent from sustainability science:

1 to understand and contribute to the design of sustainable solutions: and
2 to promote reasoning and deliberation over the meanings, goals and pursuit of sustainability.

This follows Dewey's (1938) method of inquiry, which as Minteer (2002: 43) notes, acts as 'the social process for transforming problematic situations into ones that are more settled and secure.' This method maintains a 'critical link between reflective practice – thought – and the world of lived experience' (Minteer 2002: 43) and remains open to revision and refinement as new problems arise or existing problems come to be viewed in new ways.

The vision for a new sustainability science of design presented here is empirical, normative and, most importantly, pragmatic. It is empirical in that it seeks to advance the state of knowledge about how sustainable solutions can be created and how deliberation can be enriched and facilitated. It is normative in that I argue sustainability science *ought* to meet these objectives. Finally, it is pragmatic in that the test of its effectiveness in meeting its objectives ultimately lies in changes that result in more sustainable outcomes as defined through a deliberative process *in society*.

Design of sustainable solutions

By design, I do not necessarily mean the creation and manufacture of a techno-logical artifact such as a greener building or cleaner burning fuel (though these would still qualify). Rather, following Simon (1996: 111), the process of design is the choosing of a 'course of action aimed at changing existing situations into preferred ones.' A science of design attempts to understand what the preferred or sustainable situations are and contribute to the identification and navigation of a course(s) of action that might achieve them. It is concerned with how things ought to be.

As Simon argues, the natural and social sciences have been preoccupied with how things are. As previously noted, sustainability science has also been stuck in this mode of inquiry. Research in sustainability science has focused on the 'problem space' – the understanding of current conditions and dynamics. This often comes at the expense of inquiry into preferred (i.e. more sustainable) situations and how we might get there – the 'solution space.' A design science for sustainability must move beyond analyzing how things are and engage with the question of how things ought to be. Even with a perfectly accurate and uncontested representation of the current state of affairs (which is likely to be ontologically, epistemologically and normatively impossible), the degree to which such information would lead to consensus in pursuing a common vision of the future is questionable. A design science for sustainability aims to support what Simon would call a 'satisficing' solution. In the face of real-world complexity, real-world optimization is impossi-ble. Therefore, we should aim for and accept 'good enough' alternatives that satisfice (Simon 1983, 1996). Such satisficing design solutions avoid getting stuck in in the 'knowledge-first trap' in which more knowledge is required to reduce uncertainty before action is appropriate (Sarewitz et al. 2010). They are robust in a range of possible conditions and further experience allows for learning and changes in design and action (Hickman 2001; Lee 1993; Norton 2005; Simon 1996).

Design science, argues Simon (1996), devises artifacts to attain goals. Artifacts do not necessarily have to be material objects. Following both Simon (1996) and Hickman (2001), artifacts are defined as technological objects, assemblages, institutions, knowledge and conceptual frameworks that can be used to attain desired ends. Similarly, Dewey (1920: 60) argues that theories, systems and hypo-theses are but tools whose 'value resides not in themselves but in their capacity to work shown in the consequences of their use.' Dewey (1920: 21), for instance, defines knowledge as 'purposeful, experimental action acting to reshape beliefs and institutions.' Even our futures are artifacts, which we construct and continually build and rebuild (Hickman 2001). However, as both Simon (1983, 1996) and Dewey (1920) argue, advances in inquiry into the way things are have not been matched by similar advances in inquiry into how things ought to be. It is this imbalance that sustainability science must begin to rectify.

The brief case study of the Lowell Center for Sustainable Production at Univer-sity of Massachusetts Lowell included next presents an example of how a design science for sustainability can contribute to the analysis and design of solutions through the production of artifacts (in the form of knowledge not just about the problem, but of the social system and through a demonstration of alternative solutions).

THE LOWELL CENTER FOR SUSTAINABLE PRODUCTION

The Lowell Center for Sustainable Production focuses on the redesign of production and consumption systems. Sustainable production is defined as the creation of goods and services using processes and systems that:

- do not pollute;
- conserve energy and natural resources;
- are economically viable;
- are safe and healthful for workers, communities and consumers; and
- are socially and creatively rewarding for all working people (Sustainable Production Project 2009).

The Lowell Center works with government, industry, community groups and others to develop practical solutions to environmental problems, particularly those related to occupational health and safety.

There are two core characteristics of the Center's approach that are especially relevant for a design science for sustainability. First, systems of production and consumption are viewed as both social and technological. Second, as co-Director David Kriebel notes (interview), it is important to make the distinction 'between the system in which the problem occurs and the system in which the solution occurs' or, in other words, to distinguish between the problem space and the solution space. Two brief examples serve to illustrate these points.

The Lowell Center's Sustainable Hospitals Program works to reduce or eliminate worker and patient exposure to environmental hazards while maintaining patient care and costs (see www.sustainableproduction.org/proj.shos. abou.php). Formaldehyde, a carcinogen regulated by several national, state and local government agencies, is used in many hospital laboratories for tissue preservation and fixation. A Massachusetts hospital had been served several violation notices relating to formaldehyde in its waste water, the source of which was the histopathology laboratory. Despite the installation of expensive engineering controls, violations continued. Hospital managers sought to replace formaldehyde with another chemical and a microwave oven; however, the laboratory's chief pathologist disagreed on their interpretation of the problem and argued that the managers' alternative would not allow the lab to produce the same quality of work. An alternative, glyoxal, was identified after learning of its use by a prestigious hospital nearby and a pilot study concluded that its use would maintain the quality of the laboratory practices while reducing the harmful side effects of formaldehyde (Quinn *et al.* 2006).

The second example illustrating the benefits of focusing on solutions is the conversion of dry cleaning facilities using the solvent perchloroethylene (Perc) to a water-based or 'wet cleaning' process (www.turi.org/TURI_Publications/ TURI_Chemical_Fact_Sheets/Fact_Sheet_-_Alternatives_to_Perchloroethylene_ Used_in_Professional_Garment_Care). The water-based process substantially reduces adverse human and environmental health consequences but involves significant capital investments including a full equipment replacement. Working with the Toxic Use Reduction Institute (TURI) at the Lowell Center for Sustainable Production, researchers realized that the cost of new equipment (for which the state provided financial assistance) was not the only barrier to moving away from perc use in dry cleaning. In addition to cost barriers, retraining of personnel would be required to make the switch to wet cleaning and Lowell Center and TURI researchers needed to demonstrate that the new systems would enable cleaners to grow their businesses. TURI worked with community leaders to set up sites to demonstrate the wet cleaning processes and show the public (i.e. the consumers of cleaning services) the health and economic benefits of switching away from perc and dry cleaning (Silver Hanger Case Study Brochure 2010).

In both of these cases, the nature of the problem was clear – the use of formaldehyde and perc are harmful – and alternatives were known to exist and were easily accessible. Nonetheless, the harmful practices and processes persisted. In each case, the barriers to more sustainable practices were in the solution space not in the problem-space (Sarewitz et al. 2012). Lab workers knew that formaldehyde was harmful, but did not believe that there was a viable solution that would allow them to continue their work effectively. New wet cleaning practices required effectiveness to be demonstrated, and training. Lowell Center researchers and their partners viewed each of these issues as much more than a simple technological fix – i.e. substitute glyoxal for formaldehyde and wet cleaning practices for dry cleaning. Such 'drop-in' attempts rarely work as they fail to systemically examine alternative strategies that minimize adverse consequences while achieving the desired outcome (Sustainable Production Project 2009). The critical barriers and opportunities to more sustainable outcomes were also social. It was not enough for researchers to analyze the problem and point out the harmful products and practices. Researchers, working with partners and stakeholders, demonstrated the viability of solutions (Rossi et al. 2006).

The Lowell Center case demonstrates that understanding the problem is not sufficient to overcome barriers to change towards sustainability. Systems of production and consumption are not just part of the problems, but crucial contributors to sustainable solutions. By focusing on the social and technological barriers to change, the Lowell Center is able to work with partners to identify products and practices that result in positive, more sustainable outcomes.

Reasoning and deliberation over the meanings and goals of sustainability

The objective of a sustainability science of design is not to develop more complete knowledge of underlying system dynamics that will lead to the identification of an optimal solution. Instead, it seeks to create artifacts, including knowledge and conceptual frameworks, that 'permit functional reasoning' (Simon 1996: 146). That is, it should promote and enrich purposeful deliberation over preferred or desirable outcomes – what is sustainability, what should be sustained and for whom – and how to pursue them. To some extent, existing efforts in sustainability science may serve this role. However, this proposal seeks to broaden current research in sustainability to move beyond coupled systems research and engage with the social, political and normative aspects of not just the creation of sustainability problems, but the formulation of potential solutions (Miller *et al.* 2014).

As Norton (2005: 335) argues, '...the problem of how to measure sustainability... is logically subsequent to the prior question of what commitments the relevant community is willing to make to protect a natural and cultural legacy.' Part of the role of sustainability science is to support deliberation over such commitments and, from there, help communities monitor and navigate progress. This role for sustainability science stems from a democratic understanding of sustainability as a platform for the articulation and pursuit of community goals. This also follows Dewey's own notion of democracy, which, as Minteer (2002: 41) notes, 'is not just one form of social life among other workable forms of social life; it is the precondition for the full application of intelligence to the solution of social problems.'

A design science for sustainability explores how to achieve the goals of sustainability (i.e. the 'ought') that communities and society articulate. Following Dewey and Norton (2005), design science is pragmatic in nature. It does not seek to fully characterize underlying system dynamics or define the 'right' sustainability; rather, it serves to clarify and formulate questions of practical importance that will help communities act in the world. Sustainability science must focus on constructing the necessary artifacts (e.g. deliberative space, conceptual frameworks) for discussion and dialogue over the values that ought to be sustained in a given community. Sustainability science should help to clarify and formulate questions that have practical import in the pursuit of sustainability (Norton 2005).

As Dewey (1920) notes, 'the isolation of thinking encourages the kind of observation which merely accumulates brute facts... but never inquiris into their meaning and consequences.' Thinking, for Dewey, is not just confronting facts but also involves moral, aesthetic and political reflection on the process of inquiry and into the found reality. Dewey also argues that advances in inquiry, invention and control by the biophysical sciences have not been matched by a similar command over our social and moral welfare. It is for this reason that we so often appeal to the biophysical sciences to help us solve difficult environmental problems. There is an embedded assumption by sustainability scientists that a confrontation with the facts of human–environment dynamics isolated from moral and political reflection will help to change beliefs and institutions.

For pragmatists, as Norton (2005) notes, a shared focus on real-world problems and experience unites inquiry. Inquiry here is not limited to the purely scientific kind. Rather, it is inquiry used more broadly – as Dewey (1920) employs the word – to mean a confrontation with facts by a community of inquirers and as a way to make sense of experience. In this sense, a sustainability science of design follows both Dewey and Norton in attempting to bind inquiry to experience and to ensure that it includes not only fact finding but also moral and political reflection.

Reasoning and deliberation are necessary for more than just political means – to practically achieve some predetermined end. Sustainability necessarily must be defined through democratic processes as communities engage in both fact finding and reflection about what is important. Furthermore, deliberative processes have been shown to be epistemologically and pragmatically valuable (Brown 2009; Newig *et al.* 2010; Norton 2005; Thompson *et al.* 2007). Such deliberation attempts to avoid an appeal to transcendent principles, whether they are scientific, ethical or otherwise. As Longino (1990: 141) argues, '[t]he point is that there is nothing further, that appeal to standards or methodological norms beyond those ratified by the discursive interactions of an inquiring community is an appeal to transcendent principles that inevitably turn out to be local.' Sustainability science, instead, should promote what Miller (2008) and Jasanoff (1998) refer to as *reasoning together* – a mutual learning and accommodation among people with highly divergent approaches and knowledges (Miller 2008). Deliberation is also potentially transformative, changing beliefs and values via learning and discussion (Habermas 1984; Griffith 2010).

In this way, the epistemological – how we know what we know – and the normative – what ought to be – questions of sustainability can be brought together to foster social learning (Latour 2004; Norton 2005). This approach rejects the boundary that sustainability science has drawn around a detached epistemic core, bringing together questions of epistemic and normative significance. It promotes research that is relevant to widely held social values and allows communities to evaluate the impact of their experience and values on the environment or desired futures (Norton 2005; Redman 1999). As Norton (2005: 118) argues, this 'social learning is expected to improve understanding of the environment through an iterative and ongoing process that will require not just unlimited inquiry but also the encouragement of variation in viewpoints and the continual revisiting of both scientific knowledge and articulated goals of the community.'

This objective also endorses what Verweij *et al.* (2006) call 'the case for clumsiness.' As mentioned previously, many sustainability problems – from climate change to water management – involve endemic conflict and may involve multiple understandings of the problems and potential responses. Problem-solving strategies that limit ways of knowing and social values are likely to fail in contexts where there are a diversity of definitions of the problem, needs and stakeholders (Lach *et al.* 2005). Instead, so-called 'clumsy solutions' (which are similar to what Simon would refer to as satisficing solutions) are preferable. They require deliberation and com-munication in order to develop 'creative, flexible mixes of four ways of organizing,[1] perceiving and justifying that satisfy the adherents to some ways of life more than other courses of actions, while leaving no actor worse off. As such, they alleviate social ills better than other courses of actions do' (Verweij et al. 2006: 840).

Processes of reasoning and deliberation are necessary to address many sustain-ability problems faced by society. As such, sustainability science must explore ways to contribute to these deliberative processes and enrich the debate over the mean-ing, goals and pursuit of sustainability. There is a wide literature on various modes of deliberation, including consensus conferences (Einsiedel and Eastlick 2000; Guston 1999) and citizen juries (Smith and Wales 1999; Ward et al. 2003). The concern here is not with the exact mode of deliberation; instead, it follows Dewey's (1927) concern in *The Public and Its Problems*, that there be an 'improvement in the methods and conditions of debate, discussion and persuasion' (Fischer 2000: 7).

The following case study, of the Dutch Research Institute for Transitions (DRIFT) at Erasmus University in the Netherlands, illustrates how sustainability science might be able to foster deliberation and social learning.

DRIFT: TRANSITION ARENAS AS DELIBERATIVE SPACES

DRIFT (www.drift.eur.nl/) aims to identify and facilitate transitions – changes in social (sub)systems resulting from cultural, economic, technological, behavioral, ecological and institutional developments at various scales (Rotmans and Loorbach 2009; Rotmans et al. 2001). Theoretically, DRIFT examines how transitions come into being and how to identify them. Practically, it works with stakeholders on how to envision, manage and monitor transitions.

Of particular interest to design science for sustainability are the concepts of transition management and arenas. Rotmans and Loorbach (2009: 186) define transitions management as 'a deliberative process to influence governance activities in such a way that they lead to accelerated change directed towards sustainability ambitions.' Transition arenas are experimental spaces 'in which the actors involved use social learning processes to acquire new knowledge and understanding that leads to a new perspective on a transition issue' (Rotmans and Loorbach 2008: 193). They allow a network of actors to then envision what a transition might look like (i.e. the desired sustainable goals) and establish an agenda to achieve it.

One particularly interesting example is a health-care transition program initiated in 2007 by the Dutch Ministry of Health, Welfare and Sports that included community groups, Dutch health-care sector organizations, DRIFT and others. Several transition experiments were set up to test alternative approaches that might act as possible solutions to persistent problems in health care in the Netherlands. Transition experiments included a youth-based mental-health program, in-house care for the elderly and the development of social support systems for patients. A transition arena was set up to run parallel to the transition experiments. The experiments allowed participants in the transition arena to better understand how the current health-care system operates and what strategies for change might be successful. They also identified a basic gap between the 'system' and the 'human' (Rotmans and Loorbach 2009). According to Jan Rotmans, former Director of DRIFT, the transition arena resulted in a vision for the future of health care in the Netherlands that is 'human-oriented, economically viable and socially embedded' (interview with Rotmans, 24 November 2009).

Critical to the transitions management process is the dialogue and deliberation enabled by the transition arena. This allows for information flow, articulation of values and goals, and the development and acquisition of new knowledge. Appropriate methods, tools and policies are then pursued relative to the vision for a transition. While understanding of the existing system is important, the focus is on how to shift to a more desirable system as articulated in the transition arena (Loorbach 2007). DRIFT contributes to the process by producing artifacts (including the transition arena itself) that enrich deliberation (e.g. knowledge about the current system, potential pathways) and courses of action (e.g. concrete actions and management to move towards articulated goals).

Design imperatives

There are several key characteristics, or design imperatives, for sustainability science that are necessary to position the field as a science for the design. This is *not* a proposal for a specific research agenda. Instead, these design imperatives act as guidelines for an effective sustainability science that can meet the objectives set out above (as illustrated in Figure 6.1). To address the limitations discussed in the previous chapter, the research agenda for sustainability must be expanded and refocused to meet a new set of objectives based on sustainable solutions and the fostering of public reasoning and deliberation over the goals of sustainability. I propose four design imperatives for the sustainability science research agenda. Sustainability science must be:

1   *contextual*, in its approach to sustainability problems and the design of potential solutions;
2   *plural*, taking multiple values and epistemologies into account;
3   *robust* in the formulation of its research agenda in order to remain responsive to a diverse set of sustainability issues; and
4   *reflexive*, meaning that sustainability scientists must be aware of their role in shaping the societal discourse around sustainability.

These imperatives and objectives act as a significant first step in repositioning sustainability science as a science of design.

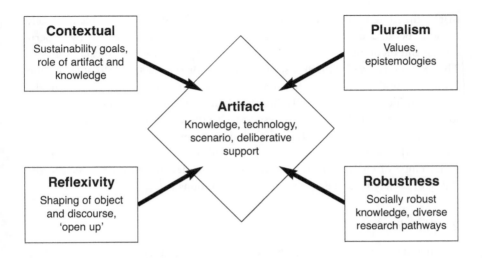

FIGURE 6.1 Design imperatives.

1   Contextual

Sustainability science must be contextual its approach to sustainability problems and in efforts to contribute to societal action. Sustainability itself is contextual – the meaning and goals of sustainability are dependent on who is involved in a given issue in a given place and what values are to be sustained (Norton 2005). Sustainability scientists have already recognized this by emphasizing place-based research (Kates *et al.* 2001; Turner *et al.* 2003a). Though it may be place-based, much of current sustainability science is not fully contextual in its approach as it is focused on producing a single type of artifact (i.e. more knowledge about the problem space) in each context.

The artifacts sustainability science devises must be contextual. First, they are dependent on specific circumstances and social practices. Artifacts (including knowledge) are contextual in the ways in which they are generated and in terms of the reality they attempt to reflect or manipulate. Second, their role in action, policy and decision making are contextual. The artifacts required to facilitate deliberation and the development of solutions will differ depending on needs specific to a given situation. As Dewey (1920: 71) argues, '[a]ction is always specific, concrete, individualized, unique. And consequently judgment as to acts to be performed must be similarly specific… How to live healthily or justly is a matter which differs with every person.' An effective design science must be contextual in its approach to the given problem (and solution) and the ways in which it seeks to foster deliberation.

This design imperative follows the concept of socially robust and contextualized knowledge developed by Nowotny *et al.* (2001). Nowotny *et al.* (2001: 168) argue that '...the more highly contextualized the knowledge, the more reliable it is likely to be... because it remains valid outside the "sterile spaces" created by experimental and theoretical science, a condition we have described as "socially robust".' This echoes Dewey's (1938) assertion that, as Brown (2009: 159) puts it, 'the "complete test" of scientific theories requires assessing their consequences in the world outside the laboratory.' Rather than being rooted in disciplinary structures, socially robust knowledge is more responsive to the values and concerns of society and is produced in conjunction with public knowledge ways, or civic epistemologies (Jasanoff 2005). It is therefore more likely to be useful to society across a wider range of circumstances. In this case, it provides the means to enhance the ability of society to design more sustainable solutions.

2 Pluralism

Sustainability science must embrace both *value* and *epistemological pluralism*. Instrumentally, pluralism must be recognized and dealt with as a means that is politically necessary to achieve desired ends. Pragmatically, this pluralism will enhance the capability of sustainability science to meet the objectives presented earlier by enabling a richer deliberation over meanings of and potential pathways to sustainability (i.e. value pluralism) and a more robust account of current problems and the consequences of future actions (i.e. epistemological pluralism). While sustainability scientists have attempted to involve stakeholders in their research, pluralism is utilized as a means to enrich the goal of enhanced understanding of coupled human–natural system dynamics (Clark and Dickson 2003; Matson 2009). Instead, argue Thompson *et al.* (1998), plurality is located in discourse, not in the multiplicity of rationally similar actors. Pluralism emerges 'in a dynamically patterned arrangement of social constructions, and in the divergent perceptions of risk and of fairness that those constructions give rise to' (Thompson *et al.* 1998: 352).

As a result of the diversity of ways in which humans interact with each other and the environment, sustainability is laden with a plurality of irreducible values (Minteer 2006; Norton 1991; O'Neill *et al.* 2008). To some, the idea of value pluralism within science is at odds with the perception of the value-free ideal of science (Douglas 2009). Yet, as science studies scholars have shown, 'there are multiple possible ends that science can serve, multiple ways in which we might want to shape our world. Not only are values part of science, but science is very much tied to society and our decisions about its future' (Douglas 2009: 53; Frank 1953). Science does not simply provide facts, but shapes our world in particular and complex ways (Douglas 2009; Jasanoff 2004b, 2005; Sarewitz 2010b). Deliberation requires value pluralism to ensure that appropriate values shape sustainability science, the artifacts it designs, and the pathways to sustainability that might be pursued. Incorporating multiple values in an explicit and transparent manner enhances democratic accountability and ensures that science addresses issues of social importance (Douglas 2009; Jasanoff 2003; Norton 2005). Value pluralism is especially important for supporting several of the four proposed design imperatives discussed below, especially reflexivity and robustness.[2]

This pluralism is also epistemic. That is, there are multiple ways of knowing the world as well as different notions of what constitutes knowledge, how it is produced and how it is applied (Miller and Erickson 2006; Miller *et al.* 2008; Rescher 2003; Healy 2003). Sustainability science must find approaches to incorporate and negotiate multiple ways of knowing, particularly civic epistemologies (Jasanoff 2005; Miller 2005), in order to develop a more robust view of current conditions and desirable futures. Furthermore, diversity significantly enhances group problem-solving abilities and improves the epistemic quality of deliberative practices (Brown 2009; Page 2007). These epistemological communities must be willing to learn from experience and are an essential aspect of sustainability because outcomes are not definable in advance but must emerge from a program of deliberation, active experimentation and learning (Miller *et al.* 2008; Norton 2005).

3   Robustness

As Simon (1996) notes, real worlds are not additive. Actions have unforeseen consequences, giving rise to new problems. We can rarely be certain that a particular sequence of actions will provide the solution that satisfies all conditions and attains all goals. Instead, in some cases it may be necessary to pursue multiple tentative paths. Robust strategies are insensitive to uncertainty about the future (Lempert and Schlesinger 2000). A robust framework asks: 'what actions should we take, given that we cannot predict the future? The answer… is that society should seek strategies that are robust against a wide range of plausible… futures' (Lempert and Schlesinger 2000: 391).

As problems emerge, change or come to be viewed in new ways, sustainability science must be adaptive in its approach. As the context changes, visions and strategies may have to be adjusted. This follows the concept of adaptive management (Lee 1993; Norton 2005), which recognizes that knowledge will rarely be certain, but that action is still necessary and so it is best to proceed on a course that might be effective over a range of possible conditions.

For sustainability science, this requires the pursuit of multiple research agendas and the exploration of alternative pathways to sustainability. The existing research agenda for sustainability science has been narrowed to focus on problem spaces. While a robust research strategy would continue research on coupled-system dynamics, it would also be part of a broader research agenda focused on sustainable outcomes.

4   Reflexivity

Reflexivity requires that a community not just respond to changing conditions but also re-examine and re-evaluate fundamental assumptions regarding desirable 'futuribles' and horizons of expectations – i.e. re-examine their very definitions of sustainability and be open to alternative articulations of sustainability.

The artifacts produced by sustainability (including knowledge) influence how sustainability challenges come to be understood by society, future research agendas and the framing of problems in complex ways (Porter 1995; Sarewitz 2010c; Smith *et al.* 2009). Therefore, it is especially important that sustainability science is fully reflexive in considering the ways it frames social understandings of sustainability – an ambiguous, contested and value-laden concept (Davison 2000; Norton 2005). Sustainability scientists must re-examine and re-evaluate their assumptions and 'open up' to alternative representations and the pluralism discussed above (Miller 2008; Miller *et al.* 2011; Stirling 2006).

Reflexivity involves attention to the representation of sustainability, its problems and proposed solutions, and the ways in which such representations end up conditioning how we view sustainability (Stirling 2006). More broadly, Grunwald (2004: 158) argues that reflexivity 'implies… a far-reaching obligation for trans-parency of sustainability research with regard to the normative premises which are employed in the production of knowledge.' These premises influence the way sustainability is represented and will influence subsequent action and condition appropriate behaviors.

Reflexivity requires openness to alternative approaches that may be more effective in advancing positive social and environmental outcomes. As Voß and Kemp (2006: 6) note, the consequence is that 'problem solving becomes paradoxical in that it is oriented towards constriction and selection to reduce complexity but is forced into expansion and amalgamation to contend with the problems it generates.' Reflexivity requires a careful balance between opening up to alternative explanations, values and representations in the design and deliberation process and closing down in order to reduce complexity and take action (Voß *et al.* 2006). A more reflexive sustainability science must respond to changing conditions and re-examine and re-evaluate funda-mental assumptions regarding the way sustainability, its problems and potential solutions are conceptualized and investigated.

The way forward

As Dewey (1920: 10) noted, eventually 'the environment does enforce a certain minimum correctness under penalty of extinction.' To date, sustainability science has focused on advancing our understanding of coupled human–natural systems. Sustainability scientists have attempted to discover the places where society might be in danger of operating beyond its limits. Such research, however, faces significant epistemic, normative and institutional challenges that limit its ability to provide useful artifacts, including knowledge, to society and is divorced from the more critical question of how to act. If sustainability science is to contribute to societal efforts to act more sustainably, a new and expanded pathway for sustainability science as a science of design is necessary.

I have proposed a new set of objectives for the field that reposition sustainability science to focus on *solutions* rather than on *problems* through the active design of sustainable outcomes and an enrichment of deliberation. Table 6.1, below, presents a breakdown of sustainability science as it has developed thus far and as a sustainability science of design. These new objectives will also advance knowledge and understanding of the social, political, natural and technological processes necessary to foster the creation of sustainable solutions. The design imperatives proposed above move sustainability science to engage the role of knowledge, both scientific and public, in social action. Each of the imperatives addresses the normative and epistemic limitations of science in the context of sustainability problems.

A design science must be contextual in terms of both the production and the use of artifacts that contribute to solutions *in context*. Value and epistemological pluralism require a diversity of perspectives and ways of knowing beyond the mere inclusion of stakeholders. Pluralism not only shapes the understanding of problems, but is critical in contributing to the design of solutions. Sustainability science must also take a more robust approach in terms of its research agenda. It must be broad enough to be useful in a wide range of contexts and substantive enough to add to our understanding of the social, political and technical processes that present either barriers or opportunities to the design of sustainable solutions. Finally, sustainability science must be reflexive in its approach to the design of solutions. As sustainability scientists move to become more engaged with sustainability and social action, they will shape the way society understands sustainability. Sustainability scientists must be careful to reflect on how they are influencing discourse and deliberation.

One looming issue is whether or not academia is capable of meeting the objectives set here, and training the next generation of sustainability scientists. A science of design requires a different and expanded skill set from those typically gained in the natural and social sciences. Miller *et al.* (2011), for example, propose that for this new breed of sustainability scientists it is not enough just to acquire substantive knowledge in a set of disciplines or problem areas; they suggest that future sustainability scientists must have a skill set that enables them to work

TABLE 6.1 Analytical focus, characteristics and objectives for potential sustainability science pathways.

	Sustainability science	*Sustainability science of design*
Analytical focus	Problem-space: coupled human-natural systems	Solution-space
Key characteristics	• Interdisciplinary • Place-based • Problem-driven	• Contextual • Plural (value and epistemic) • Robust • Reflexive
Core objectives	• Fundamental knowledge • Link knowledge to action	• Design and understanding of solutions • Foster societal deliberation in process

between science and society, be aware of the normative and value dimensions of various issues, and understand and work amongst multiple of ways of knowing, or practice what Wiek (2007) refers to as 'epistemediation.'

A sustainability science of design requires thinking beyond the current state of affairs to explore how preferred, more sustainable, futures might be developed and pursued. Institutional changes in the incentives offered to researchers, partnerships with other sectors and groups, and education must be pursued in parallel with the objectives and imperatives proposed here (Crow 2010; Miller *et al.* 2011). Just as Dewey encouraged experimentation in democracy, experimentation should also be fostered in the design of academic institutions that are performing sustainability science research and training the next generation of sustainability scientists.

From here, the next step must be to ground the objectives and imperatives that I have proposed in experience. In order to develop further the framework proposed here, exemplary case studies must be identified that have successfully generated sustainable outcomes. This will help identify certain best practices that might act as guidelines for implementing the design imperatives.

Notes

1   Cultural theory developed four ways of organizing, or plural rationalities (Douglas and Wildavsky 1983; Schwarz and Thompson 1990). These rationalities are based on myths of nature (benign; ephemeral; perverse/tolerant; capricious) and typologies of social relationships (individualist; hierarchical; egalitarian; fatalist) which map onto each other. This pluralism allows groups to hold contradictory certainties based on conflicting perceptions of the natural environment and social organization. In environmental controversies and other political spaces, it is not a question of determining 'the real risks *versus* a whole lot of misperceptions… but the clash of plural rationalities, each using impeccable logic to derive different conclusions (solution definitions) from different premises (problem definitions)' (Schwarz and Thompson 1990: 57).

2   There is much debate within environmental ethics as to whether value pluralism can accommodate the intrinsic value of nature (Minteer 1998; Norton 2009; Rolston 1994). Following Minteer (2001), I would argue that the truth-claims related to intrinsic value, while perhaps philosophically important, miss the point. The pluralism I endorse accommodates social actors that promote the intrinsic value of nature as part of a larger discourse regarding the value of and our responsibilities to nature. That is, intrinsic value exists insofar as it influences and motivates elements of social discourse and action.

References

Beck, U. 1992. *The risk society: Towards a new modernity*. London: Sage.

Benjamin, W. 2009. *On the concept of history*, pp 395–6. New York: Classic Books America.

Brown, M.B. 2009. *Science in democracy: expertise, institutions and representation*. Cambridge, MA: MIT Press.

Clark, W.C. and N.M. Dickson. 2003. Sustainability science: The emerging research program. *Proceedings of the National Academy of Sciences of the United States of America* 100(14) (July 8): 8059–61.

Crow, M.M. 2010. Organizing teaching and research to address the grand challenges of sustainable development. *BioScience* 60(7): 488–9.

Davison, A. 2000. *Technology and the contested meanings of sustainability*. Albany, NY: State University of New York Press.

Dewey, J. 1920. *Reconstruction in philosophy*. In Jo Ann Boydston, (ed.), *The middle works, vol. 12*. Carbondale, IL: Southern Illinois University Press.

Dewey, J. 1927. *The public and its problems*. Athens, OH: Swallow Press/Ohio University Press.

Dewey, J. 1938. *Logic: The theory of inquiry*. In Jo Ann Boydston, (ed.), *The later works, vol. 12*. Carbondale, IL: Southern Illinois University Press.

Douglas, H.E. 2009. *Science, policy and the value-free ideal*. Pittsburgh, PA: University of Pittsburgh Press.

Douglas, M. and A. Wildavsky 1983. *Risk and Culture: An Essay on the Selection of Technological and Environmental Dangers*. Berkeley, CA: University of California Press.

Einsiedel, E.F. and D.L. Eastlick. 2000. Consensus conferences as deliberative democracy: A communications perspective. *Science Communication* 21(4): 323–43.

Fischer, F. 2000. *Citizens, experts and the environment*. Durham, NC: Duke University Press.

Frank, P.G. 1953. The variety of reasons for the acceptance of scientific theories. In Philipp G. Frank, (ed.), *The validation of scientific theories*, New York: Collier Books.

Griffith, R. 2010. Rethinking change. In Valerie A. Brown, John A. Harris, and Jacqueline Y. Russel, (eds), *Tackling wicked problems through the transdisciplinary imagination*. Washington, DC: Earthscan.

Grunwald, A. 2004. Strategic knowledge for sustainable development: The need for reflexivity and learning at the interface between science and society. *International Journal of Foresight and Innovation Policy* 1(1/2): 150.

Guston, D.H. 1999. Evaluating the first US consensus conference: The impact of the citizens' panel on telecommunications and the future of democracy. *Science, Technology and Human Values* 24(4): 451–82.

Habermas, J. 1984. *Reason and the rationalization of society: A theory of communicative action*. Boston, MA: Beacon Press.

Healy, S. 2003. Epistemological pluralism and the 'politics of choice.' *Futures* 35(7): 689–701.

Hickman, L.A. 2001. *Philosophical tools for technological culture: Putting pragmatism to work*. Bloomington, IN: Indiana University Press.

Jasanoff, S. 1998. Harmonization: The politics of reasoning together. In R. Bal and W. Halffman, (eds), *The Politics of Chemical Risk: Scenarios for a Regulatory Future*. Dordrecht, Netherlands: Kluwer.

Jasanoff, S. 2003. Technologies of humility: Citizen participation in governing science. *Minerva* 41: 223–44.

Jasanoff, S. 2004. Ordering knowledge, ordering society. In Sheila Jasanoff, (ed.), *States of knowledge: The co-production of science and social order*, pp 13–45. New York: Routledge.

Jasanoff, S. 2005. *Designs on nature: Science and democracy in Europe and the United States*. Princeton, NJ: Princeton University Press.

Kates, R.W., W.C. Clark, R. Corell, J.M. Hall, C.C. Jaeger, I. Lowe, J.J. McCarthy, H.J. Schellnhuber, B. Bolin, N.M. Dickson, S. Faucheux, G.C. Gallopin, A. Grübler, B. Huntley, J. Jäger, N.S. Jodha, R.E. Kasperson, A. Mabogunje, P. Matson, H. Mooney, B. Moore III, T. O'Riordan, and U. Svedin. 2001. Sustainability science. *Science* 292(5517): 641–2.

Lach, D., S. Rayner, and H. Ingram. 2005. Taming the waters: Strategies to domesticate the wicked problems of water resource management. *International Journal of Water* 3(1): 1–17.

Latour, B. 2004. *Politics of nature: How to bring the sciences into democracy*. Cambridge, MA: Harvard University Press.

Lee, K.N. 1993. *Compass and gyroscope: Integrating science and politics for the environment.* Washington, DC: Island Press.

Lempert, R. and M. Schlesinger. 2000. Robust strategies for abating climate change. *Climatic Change* 45: 387–401.

Longino, H. 1990. *Science as social knowledge: Values and objectivity in scientific inquiry.* Princeton, NJ: Princeton University Press.

Loorbach, D. 2007. *Transitions management: New mode of governance for sustainable development.* Utrecht, Netherlands: International Books.

Matson, P. 2009. The sustainability transition. *Issues in Science and Technology* Summer 2009: 39–42.

Miller, C.. 2005. New civic epistemologies of quantification: Making sense of indicators of local and global sustainability. *Science, Technology and Human Values* 30(3): 403–32.

Miller, C.. 2008. Civic epistemologies: Constituting knowledge and order in political communities. *Sociology Compass* 2(6): 1896–1919.

Miller, C, and P. Erickson. 2006. The politics of bridging scales and epistemologies: Science and democracy in global environmental governance. In W.V. Reid, F. Berkes, T. Wilbanks, and D. Capistrano, (eds), *Bridging scales and knowledge systems: concepts and applications in ecosystem assessment.* Washington DC: Island Press.

Miller, T.R., and N.W. Neff. 2013. De-facto science policy in the making: How scientists shape science policy and why it matters (or, why STS and STP scholars should socialize). *Minerva,* 51(3), 295–315.

Miller, T.R., B.A. Minteer, and L. Malan. 2011. The new conservation debate: The view from practical ethics. *Biological Conservation* 144: 948–57.

Miller, T.R., T.D. Baird, C.M. Littlefield, G. Kofinas, F.S. Chapin III, and C.L. Redman. 2008. Epistemological pluralism: Reorganizing interdisciplinary research. *Ecology and Society* 13(2): 46. Available at: www.ecologyandsociety.org/vol13/iss2/art46/. [Accessed 4 August 2014.]

Miller, T.R., A. Wiek, D. Sarewitz, J. Robinson, L. Olsson, D. Kriebel, and D. Loorbach. 2014. The future of sustainability science: A solutions-oriented agenda. *Sustainability Science* 9(2): 239–46.

Minteer, B.A. 1998. No experience necessary? Foundationalism and the retreat from culture in environmental ethics. *Environmental Values* 7: 338–48.

Minteer, B.A. 2001. Intrinsic value for pragmatists? *Environmental Ethics* 23(1): 57–75.

Minteer, B.A. 2002. Deweyan democracy and environmental ethics. In Ben A. Minteer and Bob Pepperman Taylor, (eds), *Democracy and the claims of nature: Critical perspectives for a new century.* Lanham, MD: Rowman and Littlefield, pp 33–48.

Minteer, B.A. 2006. *The landscape of reform: Civic pragmatism and environmental thought in America.* Cambridge, MA: MIT Press.

Mitchell, S.D. 2009. *Unsimple truths: Science, complexity, and policy.* Chicago: University of Chicago Press.

Newig, J., D. Günther and C. Pahl-Wostl. 2010. Synapses in the network: Learning in governance networks in the context of environmental management. *Ecology and Society* 15(4): 24. Available at: www.ecologyandsociety.org/vol15/iss4/art24/. [Accessed 4 August 2014.]

Norton, B.G. 1991. *Toward unity among environmentalists.* New York: Oxford University Press.

Norton, B.G. 2005. *Sustainability: A philosophy of adaptive ecosystem management.* Chicago: University of Chicago Press.

Norton, B.G. 2009. Convergence and divergence: The convergence hypothesis twenty years later. In Ben A. Minteer, (ed.), *Nature in common? Environmental ethics and the contested foundations of environmental policy.* Philadelphia, PA: Temple University Press.

Nowotny, H., P. Scott, and M. Gibbons. 2001. *Re-thinking science: Knowledge and the public in an age of uncertainty*. Malden, MA: Polity.

O'Neill, J., A. Holland, and A. Light. 2008. *Environmental values*. New York: Routledge.

Page, S.E. 2007. *The difference: How the power of diversity creates better groups, firms, schools and societies*. Princeton, NJ: Princeton University Press.

Porter, T. 1995. *Trust in numbers: The pursuit of objectivity in science and public life*. Princeton, NJ: Princeton University Press.

Quinn, M.M., T.P. Fuller, A. Bello, and C.J. Galligan. 2006. Pollution prevention – occupational safety and health in hospitals: Alternatives and interventions. *Journal of Occupational Health and Environmental Hygiene* 3(4): 182–93.

Redman, C.L. 1999. *Human impact on ancient environments*. Tucson, AZ: The University of Arizona Press.

Rescher, N. 2003. *Epistemology: An introduction to the theory of knowledge*. Albany, NY: State University of New York Press.

Rolston, H., III. 1994. Value in nature and the nature of value. In R. Attfield and A. Bellsey, (eds), *Philosophy and Natural Environment*. Cambridge, UK: Cambridge University Press.

Rossi, M., J. Tickner, and K. Geiser. 2006. Alternatives assessment framework of the Lowell Center for Sustainable Production. Lowell Center for Sustainable Production, University of Massachusetts Lowell.

Rotmans, J., R. Kemp, and M.B.A. van Asselt. 2001. More evolution than revolution: Transition management in public policy. *Foresight* 3(1): 15–32.

Rotmans, J. and D. Loorbach. 2009. Complexity and transition management. *Journal of Industrial Ecology* 13: 184–96.

Sarewitz, D. 2010b. Against holism. In Robert Frodeman, Julie Thompson Klein, Carl Mitcham, (eds), *The Oxford Handbook of Interdisciplinarity*, Oxford, UK: Oxford University Press

Sarewitz, D. 2010c. Normal science and limits on knowledge: What we seek to know, what we choose to know, what we don't bother knowing. *Social Research* 77(3): 997–1010.

Sarewitz, D., D. Kriebel, R. Clapp, C. Crumbley, P. Hoppin, M. Jacobs, and J. Tickner. 2010. The sustainable solutions agenda. Consortium for Science, Policy and Outcomes and Lowell Center for Sustainable Production, Arizona State University and University of Massachusetts, Lowell.

Schwarz, M. and M. Thompson. 1990. *Divided we stand: Redefining politics, technology and social choice*. Philadelphia, PA: University of Pennsylvania Press.

Silver Hanger Case Study Brochure. 2010. Toxics Use Reduction Institute, University of Massachusetts Lowell.

Simon, H.A. 1983. *Reason in human affairs*. Stanford, CA: Stanford University Press.

Simon, H.A. 1996. *The sciences of the artificial*. Cambridge, MA: MIT Press.

Smith, G. and C. Wales. 1999. The theory and practice of citizens' juries. *Policy and Politics* 27(3): 295–308.

Smith, R.J., D. Verissimo, N. Leader-Williams, R.M. Cowling, and A.T. Knight. 2009. Let the locals lead. *Nature* 462: 280–81.

Stirling, A. 2006. Precaution, foresight, and sustainability: Reflection and reflexivity in the governance of science and technology. In J.P. Voß, D. Bauknecht, R. Kemp, (eds), *Reflexive Governance for Sustainable Development*. Cheltenham: Edward Elgar.

Sustainable Production Project. 2009. A new way of thinking: The Lowell Center framework for sustainable products. Lowell Center for Sustainable Production, University of Massachusetts Lowell.

Thompson, M., S. Rayner, and S. Ney. 1998. Risk and governance part II: Policy in a complex and plurally perceived world. *Government and Opposition* 33(2): 330–54.

Turner, B.L. II, P. A. Matson, J. J. McCarthy, R.W. Corell, L. Christensen, N. Eckley, G.K. Hovelsrud-Broda, J.X. Kasperson, R.E. Kasperson, A. Luers, M.L. Martello, S. Mathiesen, R. Naylor, C. Polsky, A. Pulsipher, A. Schiller, H. Selin, and N.Tyler. 2003a. Illustrating the coupled human–environment system for vulnerability analysis: Three case studies. *Proceedings of the National Academy of Sciences* 100(14): 8080–85.

Verweij, M., M. Douglas, R. Ellis, C. Engel, F. Hendriks, S. Lohmann, S. Ney, S. Rayner, and M.Thompson. 2006. Clumsy solutions for a complex world: The case of climate change. *Public Administration* 84(4): 817–43.

Voß, J.P. and R. Kemp. 2006. Sustainability and reflexive governance: Introduction. In J.P. Voß, D. Bauknecht, R. Kemp, (eds), *Reflexive Governance for Sustainable Development*. Cheltenham: Edward Elgar.

Voß, J.P., R. Kemp, and D. Bauknecht. 2006. Reflexive governance: A view on an emerging path. In J.P. Voß, D. Bauknecht, R. Kemp, (eds), *Reflexive Governance for Sustainable Development*. Cheltenham: Edward Elgar.

Ward, H., A. Norval, T. Landman, and J. Pretty. 2003. Open citizens' juries and the politics of sustainability. *Political Studies* 51(2): 282–99.

Wiek, A. 2007. Challenges of transdisciplinary research as interactive knowledge generation: Experiences from transdisciplinary case study research. *GAIA* 16(1): 52–7.

7

CONCLUSION

Sustainability and our socio-technical future

The greatest challenge facing humanity in the twenty-first century is to move our interconnected social, technological and ecological systems toward sustainability – advancing human well-being while maintaining the natural life support systems on which it depends. Nearly a quarter of a century has elapsed since the concept of sustainable development emerged on the global stage with the publication of the World Commission on Economic Development's seminal report *Our Common Future*. Since then, sustainability has captured global attention. New institutions have emerged at every scale, from global to local, and in every sector, from education to business, that is attempting to articulate a new path for social and economic progress, linking widespread concern over ecological degradation, social justice and responsibilities to future generations.

Nonetheless, the growing urgency and complexity of many problems – from climate change and biodiversity loss to ecosystem degradation and persistent poverty and inequality – continue to challenge our institutions at every level. This has led many scientists to call for research agendas that are problem-focused, applied, interdisciplinary and useful to decision making (Kates *et al.* 2011; Palmer *et al.* 2005; Reid *et al.* 2010). Scientists and the knowledge they generate have played a significant role in shaping how sustainability is understood by society and will continue to contribute to our ability to wrestle with the world's most pressing problems.

While there is little doubt that science and technology have a crucial role to play in addressing such wicked problems, there has been less attention paid to the social, ethical and political dimensions of sustainability and the dynamic between scientific research and social action in the sustainability science community. The critical question for scientists concerned with linking knowledge to action is how can knowledge be connected to actions and decision making that advance our visions of natural and social well-being? Put somewhat differently, how can science shift from identifying and describing problems to fostering the development of solutions in social and political realms?

Part I, 'Constructing sustainability science,' explored how researchers in the emerging field of sustainability science are attempting to define sustainability, establish research agendas and link the knowledge they produce to societal action. Chapters 1 and 2 reviewed the challenges the wicked problems of sustainability present to knowledge production and disciplinary organization. Science and technology studies, particularly the concepts of boundary work, co-production, and reconstruction, offer fruitful conceptual and theoretical tools for exploring how sustainability scientists frame sustainability and develop knowledge to both understand and act on sustainability problems.

Chapter 3 presents the results of an analysis of the content of the sustainability science literature and interviews with leading researchers in the field. This chapter focuses on the boundaries sustainability scientists draw around the core normative, epistemic and socio-political claims of the field. This analysis of the programs, goals and commitments of sustainability scientists grounds Chapter 4, which explores the boundaries and tensions between emerging research pathways and decision making for sustainability. There, I develop a number of insights into the implications of transforming the contested and value-laden concept of sustainability into the subject of scientific analysis.

For example, sustainability can be viewed as a platform from which communities can articulate visions of social and natural well-being, including responsibilities to nature and future generations. On one hand, science has brought many environmental problems to the world's attention, including ozone depletion, acid rain and climate change, which have in turn become the subject of normative and political concern. On the other hand, in offering objective and epistemically powerful explanations of natural phenomena, science can also constrain what is considered appropriate, legitimate or necessary discourse (Collingridge and Reeve 1986; Jasanoff 2004a; Latour 2004). Similarly, though the knowledge generated by sustainability scientists may, in theory, contribute to better decision making, the institutional and epistemological contexts that link knowledge to societal outcomes are complex and may require changes in scientific focus and practice.

Exploring these issues, Part I provides an essential understanding of the complex relationship between science, social change and the normative dimensions of sustainability. It also serves to enhance the ability of sustainability to act as a concept for articulating normative notions related to nature, social justice and future generations. Each of these points developed in Part I lays groundwork for Part II – the reconstruction of sustainability science.

Part II reformulates the sustainability science research agenda and its relationship to decision making and social action. The current approaches to investigating sustainability problems, while valuable, fall short on fostering sustainable outcomes owing to epistemic and normative limitations as well as a research agenda limited to addressing fundamental questions about coupled human–natural systems. In Chapter 5 I discuss the epistemic and normative limits of sustainability. This creates a foundation for reconsidering the role of sustainability science in the broader sustainability discourse.

Chapter 6 creates a framework for a sustainability science of design that is more overtly normative in nature, focusing on what *ought* to be in order to attain sustainability goals. It is evaluated based on its capability to frame sustainability problems and solutions in ways that make them amenable to democratic and pragmatic social action. To support this new framework, I examine two case studies of innovative sustainability research centers, the Dutch Research Institute for Transitions at Erasmus University in Rotterdam (DRIFT) and the Lowell Center for Sustainable Production at the University of Massachusetts, Lowell, that act as examples of how a science of design can be constructed. I reposition sustainability science as a 'science of design' – that is, a normative science of what *ought* to be in order to achieve certain goals – rather than a science of what *is*. This is a proposal for a sustainability science that is oriented towards the social, political and technological space in which solutions are formulated and deployed – one that aims to enrich public reasoning and deliberation while also working to generate social and technological innovations for a more sustainable future. A sustainability science of design requires thinking beyond the current state of affairs to explore how preferred, more sustainable, futures can be developed and pursued. This requires that we rethink research priorities, the role of science in society and the training of the next generation of sustainability scientists.

Transforming research and education for sustainability

As sustainability becomes the focus of new educational programs, research centers and funding agencies (not to mention a priority for global governance, urban development and the like), this project has presented a timely analysis of the emergence of sustainability science and both the opportunities and barriers faced by scientific efforts to contribute to social action. Just as importantly, it offers a framework for moving sustainability science forward with a renewed focus on innovation and the search for solutions. As such, it fills a critical gap between attempts to build research agendas focused on human–environment interactions and a better understanding of how science can effectively contribute to positive social outcomes. This project creates an opportunity for the emergence of a more reflexive sustainability science and demonstrates the necessity of addressing the social, political and normative dimensions of sustainability.

Sustainability and sustainability science, more specifically, are rapidly growing fields as evidenced by the proliferation of undergraduate and graduate programs, research institutes, funding from governmental and non-governmental sources and academic journals.

However, many of these programs carry implicit assumptions about the role of knowledge in decision making and broader social action that have been shown to be problematic. Further, these developments have largely, though certainly not exclusively, focused on the merging of insights from the natural and social sciences with the assumption that a more integrative, or holistic, understanding of sustainability problems will enable us to act more quickly and effectively. A design science for sustainability expands that focus of research to the production of artifacts that, following Dewey, can help us act in the world. Artifacts can be integrative knowledge, but can also include technologies, decision frameworks, scenarios, even stories or narratives. This design science positions sustainability science as co-creating the tools for helping communities and society to act.

This focus on artifacts has substantial implications for how research and education is organized around sustainability science. Rather than a sole concern with interdisciplinary knowledge, the focus is on the production of an artifact in the so-called solution space (i.e. the social and political context in which action might take place). It is this context that will determine the disciplines, expertise and stakeholders needed at the table; as opposed to a more abstract notion that we need natural and social sciences to understand coupled human–natural systems. As such, there must be a more fluid incorporation of engineering and technical expertise as well as knowledge from the humanities, for artifacts focused on stories, ethics or narrative scenario-building. So, too, must the boundaries between the 'real world' and academia be broken down. The ability of artifacts to contribute to substantive social action depends on their being contextualized and socially robust (i.e. valid beyond the laboratory). A co-construction of these artifacts with stakeholders, decision makers and the public is necessary to develop, test and deploy them.

Finally, these artifacts can themselves act as boundary objects (Star and Griesemer 1989), bringing together different knowledges, expertise, values and stakeholders. As the cases of DRIFT and the Lowell Center for Sustainable Production illustrate, a focus on artifacts and the solution space moves beyond disciplinary thinking to consider how sustainability goals are articulated and pursued into socio-technical systems.

As Miller *et al.* (2009: 5) note, '…the sustainability challenge is largely about how human societies in the 21st century choose to build, maintain, and reform the socio-technological systems of the future.' Sustainability transitions, however defined, will be a social, political and cultural process enabled in part by technology. While sustainability science has made substantial inroads into our understanding of complex problems in coupled human–natural systems, progress on how this knowledge will foster decisions that lead to more desirable outcomes and analyses of the processes necessary to move to sustainability are lacking. In order for sustainability science to contribute to solutions, we must pursue a design science approach. I hope this is but the beginning of an earnest and challenging discussion on new approaches and research pathways that are urgently needed to ensure a more relevant future for sustainability science and advance social-technological change towards sustainability.

References

Collingridge, D. and C. Reeve. 1986. *Science speaks to power: The role of experts in policy*. New York: St Martin's Press.

Jasanoff, S. 2004a. Ordering knowledge, ordering society. In Sheila Jasanoff, (ed.), *States of knowledge: The co-production of science and social order*. New York: Routledge.

Kates, R.W., W.C. Clark, R. Corell, J.M. Hall, C.C. Jaeger, I. Lowe, J.J. McCarthy, H.J. Schellnhuber, B. Bolin, N.M. Dickson, S. Faucheux, G.C. Gallopin, A. Grübler, B. Huntley, J. Jäger, N.S. Jodha, R.E. Kasperson, A. Mabogunje, P. Matson, H. Mooney, B. Moore III, T. O'Riordan, and U. Svedin. 2001. Sustainability science. *Science* 292(5517): 641–2.

Latour, B. 2004. *The politics of nature: How to bring the sciences into democracy*. Cambridge, MA: Harvard University Press.

Miller, C., D. Sarewitz and A. Light. 2009. *Science, technology and sustainability: Building a research agenda*. Report National Science Foundation supported workshop, September 8–9, 2008.

Palmer, M., E. Bernhardt, E. Chornesky, S. Collins, A. Dobson, C. Duke, B. Gold, R. Jacobson, S. Kingsland, R. Kranz, M. Mappin, M.L. Martinez, F. Micheli, J. Morse, M. Pace, M. Pascual, S. Palumbi, O.J. Reichman, A. Simons, A. Townsend, M. Turner. 2005. Ecological science and sustainability for the 21st century. *Frontiers in Ecology and the Environment* 3(1): 4–11.

Reid, W.V., D. Chen, L. Goldfarb, H. Hackman, Y.T. Lee, K. Mokhele, E. Ostrom, K. Raivio, J. Rockström, H.J. Schellnhuber, and A. Whyte. 2010. Earth system science for global sustainability: Grand challenges. *Science* 330: 916–17.

Star, S.L. and J.R. Griesemer. 1989. Institutional ecology, 'translations' and boundary objects: Amateurs and professionals in Berkeley's Museum of Vertebrate Zoology, 1907–39. *Social Studies of Science* 19(3): 387–420.

Appendix A
INTERVIEW SUBJECTS

Subject	Position	Interviewed	How/where
James Buizer	Science Policy Advisor to the President, Arizona State University	1.29.10	Telephone
F. Stuart (Terry) Chapin III	Professor of Ecology, University of Alaska Fairbanks	9.30.09	Gabriola Island, Canada
William C. Clark	Harvey Brooks Professor of International Science, Public Policy and Human Development, Harvard University	11.18.09	Telephone
Nancy Dickson	Co-Director, Center for International Development, Harvard University	11.13.09	Cambridge, MA
Carl Folke	Professor, Science Director, Stockholm Resilience Centre, Stockholm University	9.30.09	Gabriola Island, Canada
Mike Hulme	Professor of Climate Change, University of East Anglia	7.13.09	East Anglia, UK
Jill Jäger	Senior Researcher, Sustainable Europe Research Institute	11.18.09	Telephone
René Kemp	Professor of Innovation and Sustainable Development, Maastricht University	7.9.09	Maastricht, Netherlands
David Kriebel	Co-Director, Lowell Center for Sustainable Production, University of Massachusetts Lowell	11.16.09	Lowell, MA

Subject	Position	Interviewed	How/where
Simon Levin	Moffett Professor of Biology, Princeton University	12.16.09	Telephone
Derk Loorbach	Senior Researcher, Dutch Research Institute for Transitions, Erasmus University	7.8.09	Rotterdam, Netherlands
Donald Ludwig	Emeritus Professor, University of British Columbia	10.5.09	Vancouver, Canada
Pim Martens	Scientific Director, International Centre for Integrated Assessment and Sustainable Development, Maastricht University	7.9.09	Maastricht, Netherlands
Pamela Matson	Dean of the School of Earth Sciences, Professor of Environmental Studies, Stanford University	9.26.09	Palo Alto, CA
Takashi Mino	Professor, Department of Environmental Studies, Graduate Program in Sustainability Science, University of Tokyo	7.22.09	Tokyo, Japan
Lennart Olsson	Director, Lund University Centre for Sustainability Studies	10.30.09	Washington, DC
Elinor Ostrom	Distinguished Professor, Indiana University	9.30.09	Gabriola Island, Canada
Thomas Parris	Vice President, ISciences	7.8.09	Utrecht, Netherlands
Paul Raskin	President, Tellus Institute	12.17.09	Telephone
John Robinson	Executive Director, UBC Vancouver Sustainability Inititative, Professor, University of British Columbia	10.5.09	Vancouver, Canada
Jan Rotmans	Director, Dutch Research Institute for Transitions, Erasmus University	11.24.09	Telephone
Kazuhiko Takeuchi	Vice-Rector, United Nations University, Deputy Executive Director, Integrated Research System for Sustainability Science	7.17.09	Tokyo, Japan
B.L. Turner II	Gilbert F. White Professor of Environment and Society, School of Geographical Sciences and Urban Planning, Arizona State University	6.5.09	Tempe, AZ

Subject	Position	Interviewed	How/where
Richard Welford	Deputy Director, Corporate Environmental Governance Program, Hong Kong University	7.6.09	Utrecht, Netherlands
Jinguo (Jingle) Wu	Professor of Ecology, Evolution and Environmental Science, School of Life Sciences, Arizona State University	6.4.09	Tempe, AZ
Masaru Yarime	Associate Professor, Graduate Program in Sustainability Science, University of Tokyo	7.22.09	Tokyo, Japan

Appendix B
INTERVIEW PROTOCOL

I   **What is sustainability?**
1   To start, please describe or define what sustainability means to you.
2   Do you think that sustainability is a meaningful concept?
   i   *Prompt:* In terms of science or societal action?
   ii   Can there be multiple definitions? (Positive? Liability?)
   iii   Is it something that is achievable?
3   What are some potential barriers or obstacles to sustainability?
4   What are some of the ways you see science and technology (S&T) contributing to sustainability?

II   **Sustainability science**
1   Now I would like to turn to the role of S&T in sustainability. Sustainability has come to mean many things to many people. Please list what you consider to be the most important goals S&T should be pursuing to contribute to sustainability (i.e. what to solve).
2   What are the key research questions and priorities for S&T for sustainability that you as researchers are pursuing?
   i   What are the issues and concerns that are driving the agenda?
      1   *Prompt:* Why is this an important issue?
      2   To what extent is the S&T-for-sustainability research agenda defined by the problems it addresses?
         a   What problems? How are they defined?
   ii   What are the big problems/obstacles/challenges to addressing these issues?
   iii   What do you think the gaps in the research agenda are?
      1   Why do you think these gaps exist?
      2   How might they be addressed?
3   Does S&T for sustainability have distinct normative characteristics (e.g. what to sustain, for whom, how long)?
   i   What are they?
      1   What should they be?

     ii   What does this mean for science?

     iii   How is S&T for sustainability distinct from other approaches such as those more traditionally based in ecology or environmental science, for instance?

4   Much of the literature on S&T for sustainability stresses the importance of involving stakeholders in research and in linking knowledge to action.

     i   In your view, who is driving the S&T-for-sustainability research agenda?

         1   Who is missing from this?

         2   What is the public's role? What should it be?

         3   Do stakeholders need to be involved in S&T for sustainability?

         4   What role do scientists play in shaping research agendas for sustainability? What role should they be playing?

     ii   Has S&T been successful in linking knowledge to action?

         1   How so? Why not?

         2   What might this entail?

         3   How might S&T for sustainability influence policy more effectively?

         4   What kind of policy/action do you envision S&T affecting?

5   Do scientists involved in sustainability research have different responsibilities than those in traditional disciplines?

     i   *Prompt:* Do they have different responsibilities to science/society?

     ii   What does this entail?

6   Are there different subcommunities within the S&T-for-sustainability community?

     i   What are the differences between them? The similarities?

     ii   What would you not consider S&T for sustainability?

III Personal research and motivation

1   Please briefly describe your own research.

     i   Has sustainability shaped your own research agenda? How?

         1   How do you see sustainability making your research different?

         2   *Prompt:* How is it shaping the questions you are asking? The problems you are addressing?

     ii   Do you see your research contributing to sustainability? How?

         1   Do you consider your own work to be sustainability science?

2   How is it different from other types of interdisciplinary research (or research performed in your home discipline?)

     i   How would you identify yourself as a researcher? (What field?)

3   What has motivated you to perform research to address sustainability concerns?

4   Where would you like to see S&T for sustainability go in the next ten years?

INDEX

academic journals 16, 22
adaptive management 91
agriculture, scientification of 57–8
American Association for the Advancement of Science (AAAS) 16
Angelus Novus (Klee) 79
artifacts: co-construction, value of 102; contextual design 89–90; definition and purpose 82; deliberation process 85; reflexivity 91–2; robust strategies 91; value and epistemological pluralism 90–1
artificial sciences 80

Bali Irrigation Project 70
Beck, Ulrich 30, 79
Benjamin, Walter 79–80
Berkes, Fikret 59
boundary work: boundary management 37–8, *38*, 39; claims in sustainability science **41**, 41–2; definition and purpose 20–1; misguided by science 58; normative distancing 32, 40–1
Brundtland Report (1987) 15, 72
Bush, Vannevar 18

Cartwright, Nancy 69
civic epistemologies 49, 91
Clark, William C. 16–17, 31, 34–5, 56–7
climate science 72, 74n
clumsy solutions 86–7
constructivist approach 19–22
convergent/divergent thinking 47–8

coupled systems research 15–16, 34–5, 41–2, 71–2
cultural theory 94n

decision makers: identification of needs 37; knowledge relevance and credibility 54–6
deliberation: local knowledge dismissed 70–1; public communities 85–7; value pluralism 90
Dewey, John 67–8, 80, 81, 85, 89
Dutch Research Institute for Transitions (DRIFT) 59, 87–8

epistemic claims: boundary work **41**, 41–2; coupled systems research 34–5; social change approach 35–6
epistemological pluralism 90, 91

Folke, Carl 31
functional integrity 42
Future Earth initiative 4

German forestry science 51
Green Revolution 57, 70

horizons of expectations 73

International Council for Science (ICSU) 3–4, 14, 16

Jäger, Jill 35, 39
Jamieson, Dale 32, 41, 52

Kates, Robert 30, 32
knowledge-first trap 53–6, 82
Kriebel, David 39, 83
Kuhn, Thomas 47–8

Lansing, Stephen 70
limitations: complexity and conflicting
   guidance 69–70; knowledge-first
   approach 68, 70–1; traditional
   knowledge dismissed 58, 70; values,
   articulation of 71–3
linear model of science 18, *19*, 47
Longino, Helen 21, 52, 86
Loorbach, Derk 35–6, 39
Lowell Centre for Sustainable Production
   82–4
Lubchenco, Jane 18

Matson, Pam 32, 37, 55
medical science, selective priorities 57, 58
moral maximalism 31–2
moral minimalism 31–2

National Academy of Sciences 16
National Acid Precipitation Assessment
   Programme (NAPAP) 55–6
National Research Council (US) 15, 30,
   32–3, 72
Nelson, Richard 7, 54
normative claims: boundary work **41**;
   defining sustainability 30; procedural
   sustainability 32–3, 41; universalist
   sustainability 30–2, 40–1
Norton, Bryan G. 9, 31, 33, 41, 71, 85, 86

Olsson, Lennart 38
Our Common Journey (NRC) 15

Parris, Thomas 30, 32, 34
Pasteur's Quadrant (Stoker) 17, *17*
place-based research: case studies 16;
   fundamental element 15, 50, 54
planetary stewardship 3, 4
Planet under Pressure Conference 2012:
   State of the Planet Declaration 3–4
problem and solution space: evaluative case
   study 83–4; focus of inquiry 80, 82,
   102
procedural sustainability 32–3, 41
process-orientated approach 38–40, *40*

reconstructivist approach 23–4
reflexivity 23–4, 91–2
research agendas: academic institutions

15–16; coupled systems research 15–16,
   35–6, 41, 71–2; methodological analysis
   22; process-orientated approach 38–40,
   40; reconstructivist approach 23–4;
   science and technology studies (STS)
   19–22; social change approach 35–6,
   41; use-inspired research 16–19, *17*
Rittel, Horst 6, 10n
Robinson, John 33, 39–40
Rotmans, Jan 31, 33, 39, 88

Sagoff, Mark 42, 52
Sarewitz, Daniel 55, 57
satisficing solutions 82
science and technology studies (STS):
   constructivist analysis 19–22;
   reconstructivist approach 23–4
science of design: design imperatives
   88–92, *89*, 93; design of solutions 80–1;
   reasoning and deliberation processes
   85–7; reconstruction objectives 81,
   92–4, **93**; sustainable solutions, design of
   82–4; transition management and arenas
   87–8
scientific knowledge: certification and
   decision making 54–6; interpretation
   and contested values 47–8, 53–4, 58–9;
   perceived epistemic value 70–1, 72;
   social action, contribution to 4–5,
   39–40, *40*
Scott, James 51
Simon, Herbert 58, 80, 82
social change approach 35–6, 41
social learning 86
socially robust knowledge 89–90
socio-political claims: boundary work **41**;
   knowledge first approach 36–8, *38*;
   process-orientated approach 38–40
Stoker, Donald *17*, 17
sustainability science: core objectives
   proposed 80–1, 92–4; fundamental
   aims 5–6, 71–2; future research and
   education 101–2; institutionization of
   16; interdisciplinary research 71, 102;
   multigenerational perspective 9, 73–4,
   91; problem context 6–8, 56–7;
   tensions within 47–8; value-laden
   definitions 30
sustainability transition: scientific
   knowledge 15, 73; transition
   management 35–6, 39, 87–8
sustainable development 14–15, 24–5n
sustainable production 83–4

Takacs, David 22
tame problems 6–7, 8
technological fixes 7–8
tensions within science: constraining
    concepts and categories 50–3;
    knowledge certification and decision
    making 54–6; knowledge interpre-
    tation and social action 47–8, 53–4;
    scientizing of social problems 56–9;
    values and goals, shaping of 48–50,
    58–9
Thatcher, Peter 14
thin/thick sustainability 31–2, 40
Third World Academy of Sciences 30–1
Thompson, Paul 19, 42
Toulmin, Stephen 73
traditional knowledge: integration and
    collaboration 59; overruled by science
    57, 70

United Nations Environment Programme
    (UNEP) 14
universalist sustainability 30–2, 40–1
use-inspired research 16–19, *17*

value pluralism 90–1, 94n
values and goals, shaping of 48–50, 58–9,
    72

Walzer, Michael 31–2
Webber, Melvin 6, 10n
wicked problems: characteristics 10n;
    concept 6; interpretation difficulties 7,
    8, 69, 72
World Commission on Economic
    Development (WCED) 15, 30